TOKYO
ENCOUNTER

WENDY YANAGIHARA

Tokyo Encounter

Published by Lonely Planet Publications Pty Ltd
ABN 36 005 607 983

Australia	Head Office, Locked Bag 1, Footscray, Vic 3011
	☎ 03 8379 8000 fax 03 8379 8111
	talk2us@lonelyplanet.com.au
USA	150 Linden St, Oakland, CA 94607
	☎ 510 893 8555
	toll free 800 275 8555
	fax 510 893 8572
	info@lonelyplanet.com
UK	2nd fl, 186 City Rd
	London EC1V 2NT
	☎ 020 7106 2100 fax 020 7106 2101
	go@lonelyplanet.co.uk

The first edition was written by Wendy Yanagihara. This edition was commissioned in Lonely Planet's Oakland office and produced by: **Commissioning Editor** Emily Wolman **Coordinating Editor** Rosie Nicholson **Coordinating Cartographer** Andy Rojas **Layout Designer** Indra Kilfoyle **Managing Editor** Bruce Evans **Managing Cartographer** Alison Lyall **Cover Designer** Rebecca Dandens **Project Manager** Chris Love **Series Designers** Nic Lehman, Wendy Wright **Thanks to** Yvonne Bischofberger, David Connolly, Ruth Cosgrove, Laura Crawford, Sally Darmody, Lauren Hunt, Laura Jane, Yvonne Kirk

All images are copyright of the photographers unless otherwise indicated. Many of the images in this guide are available for licensing from **Lonely Planet Images:** www.lonelyplanetimages.com.

ISBN 978 1 74104 878 0

Printed through Colorcraft Ltd, Hong Kong.
Printed in China

Mixed Sources
Product group from well-managed forests and other controlled sources
www.fsc.org Cert no. SGS-COC-005002
© 1996 Forest Stewardship Council

HOW TO USE THIS BOOK
Colour-Coding & Maps
Colour-coding is used for symbols on maps and in the text that they relate to (eg all eating venues on the maps and in the text are given a green fork symbol). Each neighbourhood also gets its own colour, and this is used down the edge of the page and throughout that neighbourhood section.

Shaded yellow areas on the maps denote 'areas of interest' – for their historical significance, their attractive architecture or their great bars and restaurants. We encourage you to head to these areas and just start exploring!

Prices
Multiple prices listed with reviews (eg ¥10/5 or ¥10/5/20) indicate adult/child, adult/concession or adult/concession/child.

> Although the authors and Lonely Planet have taken all reasonable care in preparing this book, we make no warranty about the accuracy or completeness of its content and, to the maximum extent permitted, disclaim all liability arising from its use.

WENDY YANAGIHARA

Wendy first toured Tokyo perched on her mother's
hip at the age of two. Beyond childhood summers
spent with relatives in Japan, she has spent time
over the past several years diligently eating, drinking and dancing her way across Tokyo in the name
of research. She has contributed to several Lonely
Planet titles including *Japan*, *Tokyo*, *Vietnam*, *The
Asia Book* and *Southeast Asia on a Shoestring*. Before
pitching herself into writing for Lonely Planet in
2003, she taught English in Vietnam and worked as
a designer for publishers (including Lonely Planet)
in the San Francisco Bay Area, Santa Barbara and

Lake Tahoe. When not in Japan she continues a self-directed study of Japanese language and literature, and contemplates following in her mother's
footsteps in the study of the *koto* (a Japanese 13-stringed instrument).

WENDY'S THANKS

Much love and appreciation go to my 'Five Families' – the Maekawas,
Takahashis, Yanagiharas and two branches of Yamamotos. *Arigatō goza-
masu* to Naoya, Midori, Kenichi, Mariko and Jason for running around
town with me; to those innumerable helpful Tokyoites for their insight;
and to Mark for ineffable, irreplaceable monkeyness.

THE PHOTOGRAPHER

Growing up in Melbourne, Anthony Plummer unearthed a nest of travel
bugs. He has since dedicated years to soothing those itches, but neither
bitter Kyrgyz kumiss nor smooth Belizean Beliken beer could cure his
hankering for a peripatetic life. Perhaps even stronger than the call of the
road is Anthony's fondness for photography. His work has appeared in
various magazines and publications including Lonely Planet.

Our Readers Many thanks to the travellers who wrote to us with helpful hints, useful advice and interesting anecdotes,
including Angela Alb, Scott Allison, Damian Connolly, Jean-Louis Fragnay Chadwick Ko, Sasha Naod and Scott Stubbs.

Cover Photograph Late-night dining Shinjuku, Tokyo. James Whitlow Delano. **Internal Photographs** David Coll/OnAsia
p33; TWPhoto/Corbis p15; Iain Masterson/Alamy p84, p172; Richard T Nowitz/Corbis p157; Bernard O'Kane/Alamy p17; Peter
Usbeck/Alamy p34; Photo Japan/Alamy p30; Steve Vidler/Imagestate Ltd/Photolibrary p29; Tom Wagner/TWPhoto/Corbis
p109; Wendy Yanagihara p53, p70, p114; Haruyoshi Yamaguchi/Corbis p32, p169; Toru Yokota/OnAsia p31. All other photographs by Lonely Planet Images, and by Anthony Plummer except John Ashburne p164, p168; Antony Gibin pp10–1; Greg Elms
p6 (bottom), p12, p13, p24, p25, p27, p36 (top right), p38, p59, p65, p69, p72, p77, p73, p90, p173, p175, p181; Lou Jones
p180; Martin Moos p144; Michael Taylor p165.

A local busker strikes a chord with the crowd in Inokashira Park, Kichijōji (p92)

CONTENTS

Why is our travel information the best in the world? It's simple: our authors are passionate, dedicated travellers. They don't take freebies in exchange for positive coverage so you can be sure the advice you're given is impartial. They travel widely to all the popular spots, and off the beaten track. They don't research using just the internet or phone. They discover new places not included in any other guidebook. They personally visit thousands of hotels, restaurants, palaces, trails, galleries, temples and more. They speak with dozens of locals every day to make sure you get the kind of insider knowledge only a local could tell you. They take pride in getting all the details right, and in telling it how it is. Think you can do it? Find out how at lonelyplanet.com.

THIS IS TOKYO

Life in Tokyo moves at a well-oiled clip, with an energy that borders on mania and an obsession with newness that seems to make all ideas quickly obsolete. Fashions begin to fade almost as soon as they are plucked from clothes hangers, and *keitai* (mobile phones) are traded up for each latest technological advancement. But even while throngs of tech-savvy, smartly styled Tokyoites trot through subway stations, there is a traditional side to this hyperurban cosmopolis, which may not be immediately evident.

Beneath the conspicuous consumption of its shopping districts and shiny façades of the latest architectural achievement, Tokyo throws out unexpected glimpses of its cultural core. At a Shintō shrine across town, a young man purchases a fortune and, after reading it, ties it to a strung frame whose many paper fortunes rustle like leaves in a breeze. In a neighbourhood *sentō* (public bath) in Asakusa, an old woman bathes with her tiny granddaughter, much as she once did with her own grandmother.

Tokyo's unique vitality springs from this intertwining of the new with the time-honoured old. While it's the wellspring of Japanese pop culture, it is also a place where the patrilineage of its imperial family is a tightly held institution. It's the city to which Japanese nonconformists flee but where individuality is often linked to an older form of small-group identity. It's a metropolis where the pressure cooker of traditional societal mores and expectations explodes into cutting-edge art, music and inventions like the 'boyfriend's arm pillow'. Even pop culture like manga, as it takes the world by storm, is rooted in the tradition of Edo-period ukiyo-e (wood-block prints from the 'floating world'). And so, as its modern gears keep turning, the basic machinery of this intriguing city remains true to its origins.

Top left A traditional wedding at Meiji-jingū-gyoen (p103) **Top right** Tokyo's fashionable youth culture lets its hair down **Bottom** School kids tie their fortunes at Sensō-ji Temple (p77)

>HIGHLIGHTS

Through the spidery legs of *Maman* looms the Roppongi Hills tower (p143)

>1 THE BIG BOYS

ENJOY THE RITUALISTIC DISPLAY OF ATHLETIC PROWESS THAT IS SUMŌ

Highly ritualistic and more athletic than initial appearances may imply, sumō is a stunning, charged spectacle that you cannot miss if you're in Tokyo at tournament time. Linked with the rituals of Shintōism, sumō probably originated about 2000 years ago, but only became a popular sporting event in its own right in the 17th century. Sumō's whole visual vocabulary is infused with Shintōist motifs and ideas, from the scattering of salt to the structure and embellishments of the sumō *dōyō* (wrestling ring).

The rules are simple: the *rikishi* (wrestler) who causes any part of his opponent's body other than his feet to touch the ground inside the *dōyō*, or pushes him outside the *dōyō*, wins. Although *rikishi* may look like infants on steroids, those prodigious amounts of flesh conceal some very powerful muscle.

The action during the Tokyo tournaments, or *bashō*, takes place at the green-roofed Ryōgoku Kokugikan (p64) in January, May and

September. Although the best ringside seats are bought up by those with the right connections, box seats accommodating up to four people are a great way to watch sumō in style. Attendees in box seats can order food and tea from servers dressed smartly in *happi* (half-coats) and straw sandals.

RITUALS OF THE RING

It begins with the victor of the last match offering a wooden ladle of water to the incoming *rikishi* (wrestler), in order to perform a symbolic cleansing. Before entering the *dōyō*, each *rikishi* takes a handful of coarse salt to scatter before him to purify the ring. Then squatting, facing each other from opposite ends of the *dōyō*, they stretch their arms out to their sides, palms raised, to signify their intentions for a fair fight. Several minutes of false starts — in which they both slap their thighs and bellies in an intimidating manner — usually precede the final stare down as the *rikishi* settle into squats. Only when both *rikishi* have put both fists to the ground does the match officially begin, at which point the opponents will suddenly charge.

>2 HARAJUKU GIRLS

PLAY PAPARAZZO TO THE SUNDAY SUBCULTURE CELEBRITIES AT JINGŪ-BASHI

You don't have to show up on weekends, but then you'll miss out on Harajuku's most famed populace: the flamboyant and outrageously clad *cosplay-zoku* (costume-play gang). It's an organic rather than organised group, a constantly evolving conglomeration of mostly teenage girls, often those who are bullied in school. By inhabiting alter egos, they find freedom and acceptance in subcultures whose 'official' garb is wildly creative.

Some of the *cosplay-zoku* are fans of *visual-kei* (visual-type) bands, or of *anime* characters, which is reflected in their choice of costume; many others simply dress as a subculture's aesthetic dictates, like the vampy, black-on-black Goth-loli (Gothic Lolita). The resulting kaleido-scope of costumes ranges from *anime* superhero garb, bloody-eyed nurse outfits, blonde ringlets and Victorian bustles or over-the-top platform heels paired with postmodern kimonos. Although their get-ups run the gamut, they're united in a sense of pride in their alienation.

Weekends draw the *cosplay-zoku* from the suburbs of Tokyo to Jingū-bashi, the bridge linking Meiji-jingū (p103) with Omote-sandō (p102), – which, in turn, draw hordes of tourist-paparazzi excitedly snapping away as the girls pose, sulk and preen resplendent in all their crazy finery.

>3 TSUKIJI MARKET

DODGE FLYING FISH AT TOKYO'S WORLD-FAMOUS SEAFOOD MARKET

Come for the tuna auctions, stay for the sushi breakfast. After it's been fished from the sea and before it turns up on a sashimi platter, most of Tokyo's seafood transits through Tsukiji Market (p51). This gigantic pulsating hub of Tokyo's gastronomic system pumps at a frenetic, fish-fuelled pace. Watching the rough-and-ready, hardworking market men and women of Tsukiji, you can imagine the massive creative, communal energy that allowed Tokyo to rise, in less than 200 years, from riverside swamp to one of the world's greatest cities. But you'll have to catch this market atmosphere while you can, as the market will be relocating to new digs in 2012.

You'll have to trundle out here early to see the predawn arrival of fish and its wholesale auctioning, but even around 7am there's still some good market bustle and seafood slinging going on. Slicks of wet muck cover the floor, so don't wear your party shoes, and watch out for the electric carts zipping around the narrow aisles.

After poking around the market, move out to the nearby alleys of the external market, where hundreds of little stalls sell pottery, cooking equipment, cutlery and packaged foods for a fraction of the prices charged at department stores. Then top it all off with melt-in-your-mouth bluefin sushi as another morning winds down in Tsukiji.

>4 GOLDEN GAI

DRINK AT DUSK IN THE NARROW ALLEYS OF THE GOLDEN GAI

Tenaciously hanging on in the shadow of the skyscrapers surrounding it, the narrow alleys of the Golden Gai are a stubborn anomaly in a city relentlessly obsessed with making the old new. Filled with tiny, eccentric drinking establishments, some so small that they can only fit a few patrons at a time, these alleys come to life as dusk settles and the lights of the city begin to glow. Wandering into this little maze at this witching hour feels like walking into a time warp.

But as the keepers of older bars retire, many spots are being turned over by a new generation who are remaking them with their own creative style while honouring the spirit of these small watering holes. While it's true that some bars in the Golden Gai do not welcome foreigners, or even nonregulars, those that do are an intriguing and unique venue for a drink.

See also p97.

> 5 GHIBLI MUSEUM

GET SPIRITED AWAY TO *ANIME* MASTER HAYAO MIYAZAKI'S CHARMING MUSEUM

Fall under the spell of a Hayao Miyazaki film and you'll never be one of the philistines who liken him to a Japanese Walt Disney. Surreal landscapes, anthropomorphic objects and spirit-characters form the enticing worlds of Miyazaki's animated movies, in which the story-telling is as compelling as the phenomenally rendered animation. And though the storylines may be directed at children, they aren't saccharine or condescending, instead acknowledging the world of children as complicated yet hopeful.

A real-life testament to this way of thinking, the Ghibli Museum delights fans with its cat bus, tiny rooms and towers, cosy movie theatre and artist's studio that looks as though the animator had just stepped out and left his work on the table. Walls are papered with actual Miyazaki drawings while paints, toys and antique film projectors make up the captivating clutter of the studio. Each ticket even contains an original animation cel from a Studio Ghibli film.

See p91 for ticketing information.

>6 ROPPONGI ART TRIANGLE

MAKE THE ROUNDS OF ROPPONGI FOR A DOSE OF AU COURANT ART, ARCHITECTURE AND DESIGN

It took developer Minoru Mori 17 years to buy up the real estate he envisioned developing into what is now Roppongi Hills, an inner-city mini-metropolis. After the initial hype of its grand opening, most flock here for the shopping, but others come for the fantastic art installations and exhibitions featured in the 53rd-floor Mori Art Museum (p139; pictured above).

The Mori Art Museum created the first point in what is known as the Roppongi Art Triangle, whose other angles are anchored by the Suntory Museum (p143) and the National Art Center Tokyo (p139). Together, these three sites can make for a mammoth of a museum day, but between them they'll offer a respectable breadth of Japanese and international art spanning thousands of years. Start with one or more of the current shows at the beautifully curvaceous National Art Center, and then take lunch at Tokyo Midtown before checking out the Suntory Museum. Save the Mori Museum for last, so you can take in the glittering nighttime panorama from Tokyo City View (p139).

>7 EDO-TOKYO MUSEUM

**EXPLORE THE CAPTIVATING EXHIBITS DETAILING
EDO-ERA LIFE AT THE EDO-TOKYO MUSEUM**

The oddly modern, tradition-inspired exterior of the Edo-Tokyo
Museum (p65) both belies and reflects what's inside – exhibits illustrating Tokyo's rise from the humble riverside origins of Edo (the
Eastern capital) to today's futuristic megalopolis. The museum's
layout is imaginatively designed, with a full-size replica of the bridge
at Nihombashi dividing the vast display into recreations of Edo-
period and Meiji-period Tokyo.

Large, life-size reconstructions of typical wooden homes and workshops depict scenes from everyday living these are outdone only by
the intricately assembled scale models of the riverside near Nihombashi, the market and the residence compound of a *daimyō* (feudal
lord). Examples of the wooden wells and water pipes that made up
Edo's first waterworks system bring to life the more quotidian under-
pinnings of Edo infrastructure, while displays of the gorgeously made
kimonos worn by style-setting courtesans capture the more glamorous aspects of its culture. Don't miss the miniature animated model of
a kabuki theatre, showing how special effects were cleverly created.

Meiji-period displays trace the influence of international culture
on Tokyo, with photographs, models and multimedia presentations,
and there's a detailed exhibit on the Great Kantō Earthquake of 1923.

While you're out here, consider poking your head into the Sumō
Museum (p64) and taking a self-guided tour of the local sumō *beya*
(sumō stable).

HIGHLIGHTS

>8 GINZA

WINDOW-SHOP WITH THE LADIES WHO LUNCH ALONG THE GINZA BOULEVARDS

Ginza is classic glam, Tokyo's parallel to New York City's Fifth Avenue. With some of the priciest real estate on this planet, the boulevards are lined with serious contenders such as Chanel, Tiffany, Hermès and the big-in-Japan Louis Vuitton. Ginza is not shy about showing off its status, nor are the ladies who shop here, displaying designer-label shopping bags on delicately crooked forearms.

Shopping here is not the exclusive domain of the elite; nestled along with the purveyors of *haute couture* are wonderful stationery shops carrying fountain pens and hand-dyed handkerchiefs, Japan's department store heavies with their heavenly *depachika* (basement food halls) and handicraft shops that carry Japanese goods befitting Tokyo's traditional roots.

Neither is Ginza only about material consumption – sumptuous eye candy fills the many art and photography galleries scattered about, and restaurants here live up to the high expectations of those who haunt the neighbourhood.

Weekends in Ginza are particularly pleasant, when Chūō-dōri and some smaller cross-streets are closed to vehicles, allowing kimono-clad ladies and toddlers alike to meander peacefully in the middle of the crowded boulevard.

See also p52.

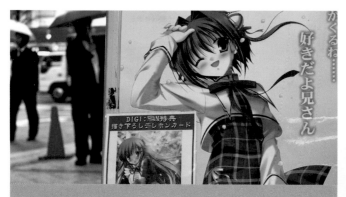

>9 ELECTRIC TOWN
GEEK OUT ON THE MANGA AND ELECTRONICS IN AKIHABARA

Don't drink too much caffeine before beginning a foray into sensory-overloaded Akihabara, otherwise known as Denki-gai (Electric Town) or Akiba. It's something akin to the maddest Asian market you've ever been in, but instead of selling mangosteens they're hawking manga and motherboards – and the sellers are not only pushy, they're prerecorded.

Once Tokyo's dominant centre for discount cameras, then videos, then computers, Akihabara's role as discount central is declining due to increased competition from huge stores in denser hubs like Shinjuku and Ikebukuro. Nowadays, Akihabara has begun to turn to the booming market in games and manga, particularly of the pornographic variety. Deals on electronics may be competitive with those of your home country but it's unusual to find prices matching those of Hong Kong or Singapore. Still, Akihabara has a massive range of electrical appliances and remains the place to find a robotic dog, wireless mouse or the most megapixels for your money.

Browse the bargain bins of games, electronics and manga and let your inner geek run wild.

See also p52.

>10 MEIJI-JINGŪ

TAKE IN THE MAGNIFICENCE OF MEIJI-JINGŪ, TOKYO'S SHRINE FOR ALL SEASONS

No doubt about it – Meiji-jingū (p103) is Tokyo's, if not Japan's, most splendid Shintō shrine. Passing under each majestic *torii* (shrine gate) takes you further into the muffled, green temple grounds to the symbolic domain of the *kami* (gods). Completed in 1920, Meiji-jingū was constructed in honour of Emperor Meiji and Empress Shōken, under whose rule Japan ended its long isolation from the outside world. Unfortunately, like much of Tokyo, it was obliterated by WWII incendiary bombing, but up it sprang again in 1958 next to Yoyogi-kōen (p28). It might be a reconstruction of the original, but it was rebuilt with all the features of a Shintō shrine preserved: the main building with Japanese cypress, and the huge *torii* with cypress from Taiwan.

On many weekends you have a fair chance of catching the striking yet subdued wedding proceedings of couples in full-on, kimono-clad regalia at Meiji-jingū. Spring brings a burst of pink when the cherry blossoms come into season, while June and July mean that the purple irises are in bloom at the adjacent Meiji-jingū-gyoen (p103), the tranquil, shaded park that was formerly an imperial garden. The one time of the year you're guaranteed not to be alone here is at New Year's and the few days thereafter, when throngs (as in millions) of people come to celebrate in Shintō style.

>11 SHIMO-KITAZAWA

DROP IN AND CHILL OUT IN THIS LOW-KEY URBAN HAVEN

The times they are a-changin' – especially in Tokyo, where it seems as though skyscrapers vanish in dust clouds and new ones sprout in their stead overnight. Sometimes this happens to entire neighbourhoods, or landmarks one would think had historical value apart from collective nostalgia.

Sadly, the meandering alleys and low-slung buildings of Shimo-kitazawa may be going the way of countless Tokyo neighbourhoods before it. The charm of Shimo-kita, a favourite of artists and hip young things, comes from its hodgepodge of tiny secondhand shops, cafés, bars and live houses. It's a world apart from the cosmopolitan centre of Tokyo precisely because of the distinct lack of skyscrapers, traffic and generic urban shininess. Street life here is pedestrian-ruled, open air, funky and human, the maze of alleys organic. The independently owned shops on either side of the station secrete incense-scented dens filled from floor to ceiling with indie designer clothing to art books and local music. In the cafés and bars, students and artists mingle with the designers and architects who have lived in this quiet haven for decades.

As construction of the Odakyū underground rail continues, so does the grassroots campaign to save the above-ground neighbourhood from being flattened by development (slated for 2010). Trek out to Shimo-kitazawa on the Keiō Inokashira line from Shibuya or the Odakyū line from Shinjuku and see if it's still humming along quietly.

>12 UENO-KŌEN & TOKYO NATIONAL MUSEUM

TAKE IN TEMPLES AND NATIONAL TREASURES AT UENO-KŌEN AND TOKYO NATIONAL MUSEUM

Expansive Ueno-kōen is one of those parks where Tokyo comes to unwind, date, have illicit encounters, busk and hone hip-hop moves. But aside from the usual attractions for relaxation, Ueno-kōen is also the place where you can coo over the pandas at Ueno Zoo, take a paddleboat for two to view the giant lotuses covering Shinobazu Pond, look in on the latest Dalí or Matisse exhibition at the National Museum of Western Art (p68) or roam around its many temples and shrines. And then there is the National Science Museum (p68), the Tokyo Metropolitan Museum of Art (p69) and the magnificent Tokyo National Museum (p69). The park packs a cultural punch.

Ueno Hill was the site of a last-ditch defence of the Tokugawa Shōgunate by about 2000 Tokugawa loyalists in 1868. They were duly dispatched by the imperial army and the new Meiji government decreed that Ueno Hill would become one of Tokyo's first parks. It's now home to these major museums and is a big destination for *hanami* (cherry-blossom viewing) in the spring.

At the park's northern end is the Tokyo National Museum, established in 1872. Comprised of five buildings, this is unquestionably

BASE CAMP

Tokyo's homeless population is estimated at more than 30,000, although government figures peg it significantly lower. Although homeless encampments exist along Tokyo riverbanks, under bridges and in isolated corners of the city's larger parks, for visitors the city's most visible homeless settlement is in Ueno-kōen. The disenfranchised population of this blue-tarp-and-cardboard tent city keeps its presence discreet during the daytime, when the park is full of visitors.

Most of these people are middle-aged and aging men who hit the skids during Japan's long economic slump. Despite their marginalised circumstances, they fastidiously hang their laundry on plastic clotheslines and line up their shoes outside their makeshift shelters, and continue to *gaman* (endure).

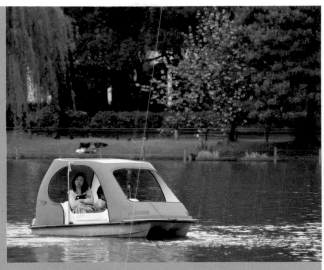

the museum of choice if a gallery stroll figures into your Ueno-kōen plans. The Honkan (Main Gallery) is the most important, with an awe-inspiring collection of art from the Jōmon period to the Edo. To the right of the ticket booth is the Tōyōkan (Gallery of Eastern Antiquities), housing art and archaeological finds from all of Asia, with an emphasis on China. To the left of the ticket booth is the cupola-capped Hyōkekan (Hyōkei Gallery), used for special exhibitions, while the Heisekan (Heisei Gallery) at the back of the complex features Japanese archaeological artefacts. Most impressive of all is the Hōryū-ji Hōmotsukan (Gallery of Hōryū-ji Treasures), featuring 300 Buddhist antiquities once belonging to Hōryū Temple in Nara. As some of these exhibits are more than a thousand years old, this wing remains closed during humid or wet weather.

The park exit from the Ueno JR station will put you directly across from the museum area, but if you take the Shinobazu exit instead, you can take in a few temples on your way to the museums.

> 13 SHIBUYA

EXPLORE WHAT MAKES YOUTH CULTURE TICK IN SHIBUYA

Schlep in any direction across Shibuya's six-way intersection for a rush of youth culture – this is *the* spot for people-watching and prime shopping. Hip *gyaru* ('gals' identifiable by their big hair, fake tans and exaggerated white eyeshadow) and their male counterparts travel in packs around Center-gai and the department stores that cater to their fast-forward fashion trends.

Leave the JR station via the Hachikō exit and you'll get an eyeful of moving images flashing across the buildings looming over Shibuya Crossing, notably the several-storeys-high screen of the Q-Front Building. Don't forget to say hello to the Hachikō statue (p120) before joining the timed tide across Shibuya Crossing.

From Hachikō exit head to the right of Shibuya 109 (p123), the streets between Bunkamura-dōri and Jingū-dōri are full of excellent youth-oriented department stores for the knee-high pink boots or vinyl micromini you covet. If you seek vinyl of a different groove, you'll hit a cluster of record shops in Udagawachō, specialising in everything from Motown to Japanese hip-hop. Also, Shibuya stays up late, and the streets between Bunkamura-dōri and Dōgenzaka are covered with clubs, bars and love hotels, so soak it up as long as you please.

>14 SUMIDA-GAWA

TAKE A LEISURELY RIDE DOWN THE SUMIDA RIVER

Travelling by *suijo-bus* (water bus, see p196) down the Sumida River not only gets you a faceful of fresh air, but brings you closer to Tokyo's riverborne heritage, showing off a more home-grown perspective of the city than a subway spin will. When you're hemmed in by concrete and glass, it's easy to forget that Tokyo's vibrant river systems are the arteries through which its commerce has traditionally flowed, from the Edo period to the present day.

Down at water level, you see the huge timber- and landfill-hauling barges, the occasional lone fisherman and the *yakata-bure* – floating restaurants where, traditionally, customers seated on tatami (woven-floor matting) eat *ayu* (sweet fish) washed down with sake. Redevelopment schemes are slowly changing the face of the riverfront, but as you pass beneath the dozen colourful bridges on your journey, you'll continue to spy the hanging laundry drying on the apartment blocks of regular Tokyo folk, as well as some prime riverfront encampments of Tokyo's more down-at-heel inhabitants.

The best way to work in a river cruise is to travel between Asakusa (p74) and Hama-rikyu-teien (p48), the lovely waterfront garden near Ginza. Consider taking in a walking tour of Asakusa sights, then catching the *suijo-bus* for a stroll through Hama-rikyū-teien. Alternatively, you could cruise across Tokyo Bay to travel from old-fashioned Asakusa out to the modern amusements of the man-made island of Odaiba (p154).

>15 SENSŌ-JI

EXPERIENCE THE MODERN LIFE OF AN ANCIENT TEMPLE

The grand old temple Sensō-ji (p77) may attract millions of tourists annually, but it is still very much a living, working temple for the people of working-class Asakusa.

Indeed, Sensō-ji's very origins are intertwined with the history of the local people. Legend has it that a golden image of Kannon, the Goddess of Compassion, was fished out of the nearby Sumida-gawa by two fishermen in AD 628. In time, a temple was built to house the image, which has remained on the same spot ever since, giving it its alternative name, Asakusa Kannon-dō. Whether the ancient image of Kannon actually exists inside is a secret. Not that this stops a steady stream of worshippers making their way up the stairs to the temple, where they cast coins, clap ceremoniously and bow in a gesture of respect.

When approaching Sensō-ji from the Asakusa subway stations, enter through Kaminarimon (Thunder Gate) between the scowling protective deities: Fūjin, the god of wind, on the right; and Raijin, the god of thunder, on the left. Near Kaminari-mon, you'll probably be wooed by *jinrikisha* (people-powered rickshaw) drivers in traditional dress with gorgeous lacquer rickshaws; these energetic, fit guides

THE MERRY *MATSURI*

You might inadvertently stumble onto a *matsuri* (festival) around Tokyo, hearing first the rhythmic chanting, *taiko* (drums) and *yokobue* (flutes) nearby, or coming across a crowd dressed in *happi* (half-coats) carrying a *mikoshi* (portable shrine) on their shoulders. If you follow the *mikoshi,* you'll eventually end up at a temple where you'll find people of all ages dressed in colourful *yukata* (cotton kimonos); stalls selling plastic toys and masks; shallow trays of goldfish to catch with a net; and, best of all, tasty *matsuri* morsels such as *takoyaki* (fried balls of octopus on a stick) and *okonomiyaki* (stuffed Japanese pancakes).

The *matsuri* is an integral part of Japanese culture, dating back to the early days of communal rice cultivation, when townships would gather to pacify the gods. Call the Tokyo Tourist Information Center (TIC; p202) for *matsuri* information.

will cart you around the temple and neighbourhood, giving you the scoop on architecture and history in English or Japanese.

Straight on through the gate is Nakamise-dōri, a busy pedestrian shopping street set within the actual temple precinct. Everything from tourist trinkets to genuine Edo-style crafts are sold here; there's even a shop selling the elaborate wigs that are worn with kimonos.

Nakamise-dōri leads to the main temple compound. In front of the temple is a large incense cauldron, whose smoke is said to bestow health. If any part of your body – modesty permitting, naturally – is giving you trouble, do as the locals do and fan some smoke your way, rubbing it through your clothes into the area that ails you.

>16 YOYOGI-KŌEN

**WANDER INTO YOYOGI-KŌEN ON WEEKENDS FOR
A MIXED BAG OF FREE ENTERTAINMENT**

Amazing but true: those Japanese rockabilly cats with their greaser
pompadours or nouveau poodle skirts still cut a rug on Sundays at
Yoyogi-kōen (p107-8), the 54-hectare city park. Bring a *bentō* and have
yourself a picnic – take your pick of background music, whether it's
shamisen (three-stringed lute) practice or a punk rock set. You never
know what you'll get for entertainment – it might be anything from
fire-eaters to pavement theatre, J-hop dance troupes to drum circles.

Officially the authorities put the kibosh on live music and dancers,
but on most fair-weather Sundays you'll find a healthy sampling of
both. The park isn't in itself all that remarkable, although walking the
lovely tree-lined paths is pleasantly punctuated by little tykes zipping
by on rented bikes. Cherry blossoms do bloom here in the spring, but
autumn is the time to come, when the gingko leaves go golden.

An afternoon at Yoyogi park could easily round out a Sunday visiting Meiji-jingū (p20), snapping pics of *cosplay* kids at Jingū-bashi (p12)
and browsing teenybopper fashion down Takeshita-dōri (p108).

>TOKYO DIARY

As one of the brighter stars of Asia's constellation of cities, Tokyo plays host to many international festivals and events. Festivities across the city can be as humble as the neighbourhood *matsuri* (p26) to huge *anime* trade fairs, gay-and-lesbian film festivals and singularly Japanese holidays when it seems the entire population of Tokyo is converging all at once on its most famous shrines. The larger holidays celebrate auspicious ages and the turning of seasons, reconnecting Tokyoites to their roots and allowing visitors a chance to mingle with locals at their most traditional.

Smiling faces and bright kimonos celebrate Shichi-Go-San (7-5-3), a festival for these milestone ages (p34)

JANUARY

Shōgatsu

From 1–3 January people turn out in droves to shrines and temples such as Sensō-ji (p77) and Meiji-jingū (p103) to celebrate the New Year.

Seijin-no-Hi (Coming-of-Age Day)

Also at Meiji-jingū (p103), traditional archery displays are held on 15 January to mark the move into adulthood.

FEBRUARY

Setsubun

At home and at temples such as Sensō-ji (p77), beans are thrown outside as people shout, 'Oni wa soto! Fuku wa uchi!' ('Devils out! Fortune in!'), to mark the first day of spring on 3 or 4 February.

MARCH

Hina Matsuri (Girls' Day)

On 3 March a doll festival is held near Azumabashi and *hina* (princess) dolls are displayed in homes and public spaces.

Tokyo International Anime Fair

www.tokyoanime.jp/en

Held in late March or early April, this huge trade fair is held at Tokyo Big Sight (p157) for *anime* fans and industry pros alike.

Hina (princess) dolls are displayed for the 'princess' in every family on the annual Girls' Day

Get as close as you dare to the tattooed flesh and tense stares of a *yakuza* gang during Sanja Matsuri

APRIL

Hanami

In late March and early April, *hanami* (cherry blossom) viewing parties (p91) take place day and night in parks across the city.

Art Fair Tokyo

www.artfairtokyo.com

Held at the appropriately innovative Tokyo International Forum (p51), this young fair showcases cutting-edge art from Japan, Asia and beyond. Artists and collectors meet here in mid-April.

MAY

Otoko-no-Hi (Boys' Day)

Family homes honour their sons by flying *koinobori* (banners in the shape of a carp) on 5 May.

Sanja Matsuri

Hundreds of *mikoshi* (portable shrines) are carried through the thronged streets around Sensō-ji (p77) over three days in mid-May.

Design Festa

www.designfesta.com

In mid-May a wide showcase of work from budding designers and artists is displayed at Design Festa, held at Tokyo Big Sight (p157).

TOKYO DIARY

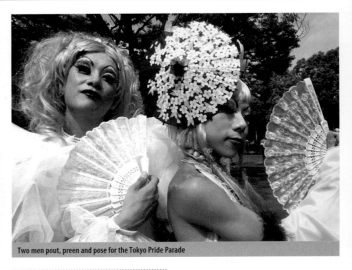

Two men pout, preen and pose for the Tokyo Pride Parade

JUNE

Iris Viewing

The inner garden at Meiji-jingū (p103) is a favoured spot for viewing irises – most vibrant in June, when these flowers are in full bloom.

JULY

Fuji Rock Festival

http://fujirockfestival.com

This outdoor concert in late July draws international acts and thousands of fans to its beautiful woodland surroundings.

Tokyo International Lesbian & Gay Film Festival

www.tokyo-lgff.org

Check the website to see where screenings are held for this queer film festival, growing steadily into its second decade. Held in mid-July.

Sumida River Fireworks

On the last Saturday of July, *hanabi* (fireworks) over the Sumida River are the year's most popular.

AUGUST

Asakusa Samba Festival

The highlight of this festival is the parade down Kaminarimon-dōri, drawing half a million spectators and samba troupes from Tokyo to Rio. On the last Saturday of August.

Tokyo Pride Parade

http://parade.tokyo-pride.org

It's on again, off again, but come mid-August, the parade may be taking to the streets in Harajuku (p102). Check the website.

SEPTEMBER

Ningyō-kujō

Dolls are offered to Kannon (the Buddhist goddess of mercy) at Kiyomizu Kannon-dō (p68) by childless couples who wish to conceive. The dolls are ceremonially burned there on 25 September.

OCTOBER

Tokyo International Film Festival

www.tiff-jp.net

This festival lasts about 10 days and begins in late October. Although featured films focus on Asia, most are subtitled in English.

Kōyō

Autumn foliage-viewing season (p175) begins in mid-October or early November. As this colourful season is longer, the crowds are more low-key than for hanami (p31).

Crowding for a glimpse of their idols at the opening ceremony of the Tokyo International Film Festival

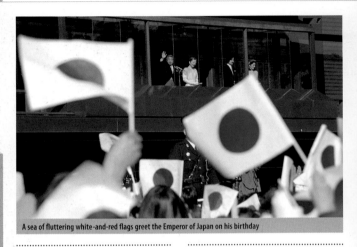

A sea of fluttering white-and-red flags greet the Emperor of Japan on his birthday

NOVEMBER

Shichi-Go-San (Seven-Five-Three Festival)

On 15 November this festival celebrates these milestone ages, and parents in turn bring their traditionally clad little ones to temples and shrines to mark the occasion on the nearest weekend.

Design Festa

www.designfesta.com

Returning to Tokyo Big Sight (p157) for its biannual stint (see p31).

DECEMBER

Emperor's Birthday

On 23 December, this is one of only two days per year that the *Kōkyo* (Imperial Palace; Map pp46–7) is opened to the public; the other is 2 January.

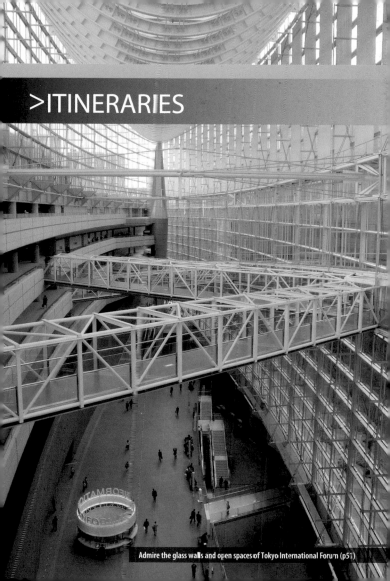

Admire the glass walls and open spaces of Tokyo International Forum (p51)

ITINERARIES

Don't be daunted by Tokyo's immensity. Taken in small bites you can get your fill of a thousand of the city's unique flavours. Pick a few must-do experiences and appealing neighbourhoods to explore. If your time is limited, use these itineraries as suggestions and customise according to your own tastes.

ONE DAY

Start at dawn to check out the catch of the day at Tsukiji Market (p13). Breakfast on the freshest tuna at Daiwa Sushi (p59), and detour through Hama-Rikyū-Teien (p48) before walking up to Ginza (p45) for window-shopping and gallery-hopping. Go underground to one of the *depachika* (department-store food basements; p57) to marvel at the gourmet goods, then play with high-tech gadgets at the Sony Building (p50). Stop for lunch at Tokyo International Forum (p51). Stroll through the Imperial Palace East Garden (p48) and exit from the garden's northeast to wander through Kitanomaru-kōen. Continue west on to Yasukuni-jinja (p51). Catch a train from Ichigaya Station to Shinjuku (p88) for an extravagant dinner at New York Grill (p96).

SUNDAYS

Pick up a *bentō* (boxed meal) and hop the JR Yamanote line to Harajuku (p102) when the *cosplay-zoku* (costume-play gang; p129) come out in force. After you've taken your 100 photos, head across Jingū-bashi to magnificent Meiji-jingū (p103). Exit the temple grounds and head west until you reach the entrance to Yoyogi-kōen (p107). Have a picnic lunch in the park. Afterwards, head back out and backtrack to Omote-sandō (p102) to while away an afternoon shopping on the boulevard and in the alleys. Treat yourself to a fusion dinner at stylish Fujimamas (p112), and end with a cocktail with the locals at Tokyo Apartment Café (p116).

THREE DAYS

Follow the one-day itinerary and then, if your visit doesn't fall on a Sunday, spend your second day on the Sunday sights but skip Yoyogi-kōen.

Top left Take to the streets on a rickshaw (p74) ride in Asakusa **Top right** Ornate doorways at Meji-jingū Shrine (p103) **Bottom** Soak up serenity with a foot bath at Oedo Onsen Monogatari (p159)

On your third day start at Hama-rikyū-teien (p48) before catching a
Sumida River cruise to Asakusa (p76). Visit Sensō-ji (p77), take a *jinrikisha*
(rickshaw) tour (p74) and bang on a few drums at Taikokan (p77). Then
walk westward to Kappabashi-dōri (p78) to check out plastic food and
kitchenware before catching the metro from Tawaramachi to Ueno (p66).
Walk through the south end of Ueno-kōen (p68) taking in the temples
and park life. Wind up at the Tokyo National Museum (p69). In the
evening, take the Yamanote line to Ebisu (p130) for dinner and a drink.

FIVE DAYS

After three days, take it easy and immerse yourself in crowd culture with
a roll around Shinjuku (p88), getting a look from the crow's nest at the
top of the Tokyo Metropolitan Government Offices (p91). Make sure to
ease into a *sentō* (public bath) or *onsen* (hot spring; p176), perhaps in
Odaiba (p154), where you can also view Tokyo from across the bay. Take
the time to check out one of Tokyo's outlying neighbourhoods, such as
Kichijōji (p92) and Ryōgoku (p64), and save Friday or Saturday for pulling
an all-nighter in Roppongi (p138).

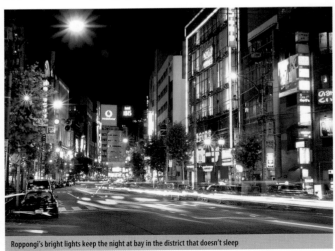

Roppongi's bright lights keep the night at bay in the district that doesn't sleep

FORWARD PLANNING
Two to three months before you go Book an appointment for the Ghibli Museum (p91); reserve a table at L'Osier (p60) to sweep your date off their feet with fancy French or at Kikunoi (p147) for memorable *kaiseki* (multicourse traditional Japanese).
One month before you go Find out what holidays (p29) will be in swing during your visit, like *hanami* (cherry-blossom viewing) in spring, Asakusa's Sanja Matsuri in May and *hanabi* (fireworks) over the Sumida River in July.
One week before you go Check *Metropolis* online (p159) for current goings-on and concert listings.
One day before you go Reconfirm your flight, review the Japanese names of your favourite sushi and pack some comfortable (and stylin') shoes.

RAINY DAY

It's wet, but this doesn't have to dampen your mood as there's lots to do indoors. Hole up in one of Tokyo's megamalls for the day. At Roppongi Hills take in a movie in the plush Toho Cinemas Roppongi Hills (p153). Have lunch and window-shop in the shopping complex before seeing the latest exhibition at Mori Art Museum (p139). End with a cocktail at Maduro (p150).

Otherwise, pretend you're in Hong Kong at Daiba Little Hong Kong (p158) and then trick your senses on the virtual-reality rides at Sega's Tokyo Joypolis (p159). Let your day end in Edo times at Oedo Onsen Monogatari (p159) with a soul-reviving soak.

FOR FREE

The budget can quickly be exceeded on unplanned expenditures like that must-have, one-off shirt you found in Ura-Hara (p102). But with the exception of Shinjuku-gyōen (p91), Tokyo's large parks are free – take your bentō to Ueno-kōen (p27) or the Imperial Palace East Garden (p48) and have a picnic. Showrooms like the Sony Building (p50) and Toyota Amlux (p84) offer up their wares for playing and testing. Roaming Tsukiji Market (p13) is a pleasure you won't pay for, as are the temples and shrines (p177) of Tokyo.

>NEIGHBOURHOODS

View from Tokyo Tower (p143), Central Tokyo

NEIGHBOURHOODS

Less a chaotic urban jungle than a massive, neatly manicured garden, Tokyo is more navigable than first glances at the skyscrapers and subway maps may have you believe. Think of its various districts as smaller villages within the bigger metropolis, for this is how Tokyo evolved and how its neighbourhoods are organised.

Most of Tokyo's action takes place around the loop of the JR Yamanote line, which encircles the central area of this sprawling city. As defined here, Central Tokyo encompasses several districts surrounding Tokyo Station, a transport hub near the Imperial Palace and the upscale commercial district of Ginza. North of Central Tokyo is Ueno, where Tokyo's largest park contains several museums and temples. Off the Yamanote orbit, to the east of Ueno, lies Asakusa, the heart of old Shitamachi (Edo's low town) with its famous temple. Out west, Ikebukuro has its intriguing corners, while further south the neon glows and skyscrapers of Shinjuku stand tall. Next stop, Harajuku, where role-play is a living art, just up the boulevard from elegant Aoyama, where high fashion reigns. But youth culture rules another stop south at Shibuya, a neighbourhood that serves up disposable style-of-the-moment. To the south, a refined but relaxed vibe prevails in stylish Ebisu and Daikanyama. Moving west, just inside the Yamanote loop, Roppongi has long been the place to party but has also gained a measure of respectability with the addition of its city-within-a-city, Roppongi Hills. Its neighbour, Akasaka, stands slightly aloof from this decadence, as the serious business of the national government is based here. Meanwhile, the loop swoops north again to Ginza via Shimbashi. It's forgivable to forget that Tokyo is a seaside city, but a visit to Odaiba, an artificial island in Tokyo Bay, makes an excellent reminder.

>CENTRAL TOKYO

Central Tokyo is rooted in the location of the Imperial Palace, where the imperial family resides today, and the outer garden on which visitors can stroll. Just across the moat is the business district of Marunouchi, where salarymen busily power the banks, communications and big businesses lining these streets. To the east of Marunouchi is the hub that is Tokyo Station, and still eastward is Nihombashi and its commerce. South of Tokyo Station lies the upscale shopping district of Ginza, whose Western architecture was once the pinnacle of modernity and now provides a stately backdrop to conspicuous consumption. Further southeast of Ginza you'll find the seafood-trading bustle of Tsukiji Market, and the revitalised commercial district of Shiodome, with its luxury hotel-and-dining complexes. The core of Central Tokyo is fringed with sights worth the walk or extra subway stop, such as the Yasukuni-jinja war memorial and Tokyo Dome for sports-mad fans, as well as specialty neighbourhoods such as Jimbōchō with its bookshops, and Akihabara for manga and electronics.

CENTRAL TOKYO

Please see over for map

◉ SEE

◉ CRIMINOLOGY MUSEUM OF MEIJI UNIVERSITY

明治大学博物館刑事

☎ 3296 4431; 3F, Daigaku Kaikan, 1-1 Kanda Surugadai, Chiyoda-ku; admission free; ◷ 10am-4.30pm Mon-Fri, 10am-12.30pm Sat; 🚃 Chūō & Sōbu lines to Ochanomizu (Ochanomizu exit), ◉ Marunouchi line to Ochanomizu (exit B1); ♿

Covering centuries of crime and punishment in Japan, this museum will fascinate both the criminally minded and the morbidly curious. While there isn't much English signage, the wood-block prints and torture devices are self-explanatory. From the stations, walk downhill on Meidai-dōri. The Daigaku Kaikan building will be on your right, on the corner just before the huge Meiji University building.

◉ GINZA GRAPHIC GALLERY

ギンザグラフィックギャラリー

☎ 3571 5206; www.dnp.co.jp/gallery/ggg/index_e.html; 1F, DNP Ginza Bldg, 7-7-2 Ginza, Chūō-ku; admission free; ◷ 11am-7pm Mon-Fri, 11am-6pm Sat; ◉ Ginza, Hibiya & Marunouchi lines to Ginza (exits A1 & A2); ♿

WORTH THE TRIP

Nestled just above Central Tokyo but seemingly from another decade, **Kagurazaka** (🚃 Chūō line to Iidabashi (east exit), ◉ Namboku, Tōzai, Yūrakuchō & Toei Ōedo lines to Iidabashi (exit B3)) is a formerly vibrant geisha quarter, whose local residents are attempting to preserve its old-fashioned integrity. Before WWII the alleys here – many of them still cobbled – saw steady foot traffic to the many traditional, exclusive restaurants called *ryotei*. Nowadays, the slope is looking almost as modern as other low-scale Tokyo neighbourhoods, with the addition of convenience stores and a few high-rise apartment buildings. But these narrow, winding alleys still hide small temples and shrines, tiny old-fashioned bars, atmospheric restaurants and its inherent, abundant charm.

Kagurazaka-dōri leads uphill from Iidabashi Station, leaving behind the canal that was formerly the outermost moat of the Imperial Palace grounds. Walking uphill, the street is lined with shops selling *geta* (wooden sandals worn with kimono), kitchen wares and old-fashioned *wagashi* (sweets). On your left is a red temple called **Bishamonten** (its formal name is Zenkoku-ji). Once you arrive at the temple, duck into the alleys on the other side of Kagurazaka-dōri to roam the winding back streets. If you continue up Kagurazaka-dōri past the main intersection, you'll eventually hit Kagurazaka station on the Tōzai subway line, which can take you back to Central Tokyo. Alternatively, you could head back down the slope and enjoy a drink along the green canal at the **Canal Café** (☎ 3260 8068; 1-9 Kagurazaka, Shinjuku-ku; ◷ 11am-10.30pm Tue-Sun; ◉ Namboku, Tōzai, Yūrakuchō & Toei Ōedo lines to Iidabashi exit B3) before leaving from Iidabashi Station.

NEIGHBOURHOODS

CENTRAL TOKYO

Excellent exhibitions with an emphasis on graphic design are this gallery's forte. The gallery also hosts workshops and talks by visiting artists, covering everything from tiny typography to monumental architecture.

☉ HAMA-RIKYŪ-TEIEN 浜離宮庭園

☎ 3541 0200; admission ¥300/150; ⏱ 9am-5pm; ⊕ Toei Ōedo line to Tsukiji-shijō (exit A2); ♿

The shōguns used to have this magnificent place to themselves when it was Hama Rikyū, 'the beach palace'. Now mere mortals can enjoy this wonderful garden, one of Tokyo's best. Sometimes known as the Detached Palace Garden, it is impossibly elegant and a must for garden aficionados. Consider approaching it from Asakusa via the Sumida-gawa cruise (p25).

☉ IDEMITSU ART MUSEUM 出光美術館

☎ 3213 9402; 9F, Teigeki Bldg, 3-1-1 Marunouchi, Chiyoda-ku; admission ¥1000/700/200; ⏱ 10am-5pm Sun-Thu, 10am-7pm Fri ⊕ Chiyoda & Toei Mita lines to Hibiya (exits A1 & B3); ♿

Most famous for its collection of work by the Zen monk Sengai, this superb, eclectic collection of Chinese and Japanese art is brought

to you courtesy of a petroleum zillionaire. There are also lovely views of the Imperial Palace from the museum, which is next to the Imperial Theatre.

☉ IMPERIAL PALACE EAST GARDEN 皇居東御苑

☎ 3213 2050; admission free; ⏱ 9am-4.30pm Tue-Thu, Sat & Sun Mar-Oct, 9am-4pm Nov-Feb; ⊕ Chiyoda, Hanzōmon, Marunouchi & Tōzai lines to Ōtemachi (exits C10 & C13b); ♿

One of the nearest emergency exits from Ginza street chaos, this garden (known as the Kōkyo Higashi Gyoen) is the only quarter of the palace proper that is open to the public. The Edo-period watchtower, Fujimi-yagura, was designed to provide the aristocracy with a handy view of Mt Fuji. The store inside the garden sells a good map for ¥150.

RUN AWAY

Runners, rejoice – there are parks aplenty in Tokyo for jogs and power walks. Our favourite is the 5km route around the Imperial Palace East Garden (above), but other great places to run include Yoyogi-kōen (p107), Jingū-gaien (p107), and Shinjuku-gyōen (p91).

Of course, for a different kind of runner's high, those top-end hotel treadmills have the most pulse-racing views.

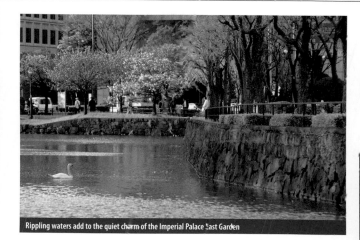
Rippling waters add to the quiet charm of the Imperial Palace East Garden

KITE MUSEUM
凧の博物館

☎ 3271 2465; www.tako.gr.jp/eng
/museums_e/tokyo_e.html; 5F, Taimeikan
Bldg, 1-12-10 Nihombashi, Chūō-ku;
admission ¥200/100; ☒ 11am-5pm
Mon-Sat; ☺ Ginza, Tōzai & Toei Asakusa
lines to Nihombashi (exit C5); &

This unusual little museum feels
like a kitemaker's store cupboard,
with everything crammed in tight
(and not much explanatory material). But the kites are wonderful, especially the vintage ones
depicting folk tales and kabuki
(stylised Japanese theatre). Made
of bamboo and *washi* (handmade
paper), the kites for sale make
beautiful souvenirs.

KOISHIKAWA KŌRAKUEN
小石川後楽園

☎ 3811 3015; 1-6-6 Kōraku,
Bunkyō-ku; admission ¥300/free;
☒ 9am-5pm; ☺ Namboku, Tōzai,
Yūrakuchō & Toei Ōedo lines to
Iidabashi (exits C3 & 6); &

A beautiful amalgam of Japanese
and Chinese landscape design,
this mid-17th-century garden is
left off most tourist itineraries.
That's a shame, because it's one
of Tokyo's best gardens; but then
again, it's also a blessing, since
you'll be far from the maddening
crowds. You can buy an excellent
English map at the garden's
entrance.

🄲 LEICA GINZA SALON
ライカ銀座店

☎ 6215 7070; www.leica-camera.us /culture/galeries/gallery_tokyo; 1F & 2F, Tokaido Bldg, 6-4-1 Ginza, Chūō-ku; admission free; ⏰ 11am-7pm Tue-Sun; Ⓜ Ginza, Hibiya & Marunouchi lines to Ginza (exit C2)

Exhibiting the outstanding work of up-and-coming photographers and long-time professionals, this clean, minimalist salon remains one of the best photography galleries in the area.

🄲 NATIONAL MUSEUM OF MODERN ART
国立近代美術館

☎ 5777 8600; www.momat.go.jp /english; 3-1 Kitanomaru-kōen, Chūō-ku; admission ¥420/130/70; ⏰ 10am-5pm Tue-Thu, Sat & Sun; 10am-8pm Fri; Ⓜ Tōzai line to Takebashi (exit 1a); ♿

The National Museum of Modern Art has a magnificent collection of Japanese art from the Meiji period onwards. Your ticket (hold on to the stub) gives you free admission to the nearby Crafts Gallery, which houses ceramics, lacquerware and dolls.

🄲 SHISEIDO GALLERY
資生堂ギャラリー

☎ 3572 3901; www.shiseido.co.jp/e /gallery/html; B1F, Tokyo Ginza Shiseido Bldg, 8-8-3 Ginza, Chūō-ku; admission free; ⏰ 11am-7pm Tue-Sat, 11am-6pm Sun; ⬛ JR Yamanote line to Shimbashi (Ginza exit), Ⓜ Ginza line to Shimbashi (exits 1 & 2)

Open since 1919, this gallery is one of the oldest in the neigh-bourhood. Showing an ever-changing selection of art, its exhibitions lean more towards the experimental and are well worth a look.

🄲 SONY BUILDING
ソニービル

☎ 3573 2371; www.sonybuilding.jp; 5-3-1 Ginza, Chūō-ku; admission free; ⏰ 11am-7pm; Ⓜ Ginza, Hibiya, Marunouchi line to Ginza (exit B9)

Although essentially a Sony showroom, this place has fasci-nating hands-on displays of Sony's latest gizmos and gadgets – some that have yet to be released. There's often a bit of a wait, but it's a good place to test-drive Sony's latest digital cameras, laptops and idio-syncratic electronic 'pets'.

🖸 TOKYO INTERNATIONAL FORUM
東京国際フォーラム

☎ 5221 9000; www.t-i-forum.co.jp/english; 3-5-1 Marunouchi, Chiyoda-ku; admission free; ⏱ 8am-11pm; 🚇 JR Yamanote line to Yūrakuchō (main exit), 🚇 Yūrakuchō line to Yūrakuchō (exit A4b); ♿

Designed by architect Rafael Viñoly, the Tokyo International Forum looks like a fantastic glass ship plying the urban waters of central Tokyo. Largely used for conventions and meetings, the cantilevered spaces and plaza also house a library, art gallery, café and shops.

🖸 TSUKIJI MARKET 築地市場

☎ 3541 2640; www.tsukiji-market.or.jp; 5-2 Tsukiji, Chūō-ku; ⏱ closed some Mon & Wed, Sun & public holidays; 🚇 Toei Ōedo line to Tsukiji-Shijō (exits 1 & 2)

Tsukiji keeps market hours, so come early for the best action – 3am is when it opens and the fish are hauled in, but even around 8am you can still get a feel for the sheer scale and energy of this phenomenal fish market. See also the boxed text below.

🖸 YASUKUNI-JINJA
靖国神社

☎ 3261 8326; www.yasukuni.or.jp/english; 3-1-1 Kudan-kita, Chiyoda-ku; admission free; ⏱ 9.30am-5.30pm Mar-Oct, 9.30am-5pm Nov-Feb; 🚇 Hanzōmon, Tōzai & Toei Shinjuku lines to Kudanshita (exits 1 & 2); ♿

Yasukuni-jinja, the perennial fly-in-the-chardonnay in Japan-Asia relations, is the 'Peaceful Country

CHANGES AT TSUKIJI

In December 2008 metropolitan officials placed a month-long ban on visitors at the Tsukiji Market tuna auctions, the alleged reason being foreign tourists acting badly. While this may or may not be a legitimate complaint, it's true that the sellers and buyers involved in the auctions have long accommodated the presence of visitors in their daily tuna transactions. Unfortunately, it seems that enough visitors overstep the bounds of polite observation to interfere with auction operations.

At press time, the ban is temporary, and visitors are still free to explore Tsukiji Market as usual. But the ban serves as a reminder that tuna is very serious business here – if you visit the auction, conduct yourself with common-sense courtesy: observe quietly from the back, don't use flash photography, and keep your hands off the fish.

WORTH THE TRIP

Tokyo Disneyland (☎ 045-683 3777; www.tokyodisneyresort.co.jp; 1-1 Maihama, Urayasu-shi, Chiba; one-day passport ¥5800/5000/3900; ⏰ vary, see website; 🚃 Keiyō line to Maihama (main exit); 🅿 ♿), much beloved by the Japanese, is a near-perfect replica of the California original…making it the second-happiest place on earth? Adjacent to Tokyo Disneyland is Tokyo DisneySea, the more maritime- and futuristic-themed sibling of these twin amusement parks, which will probably appeal more to adults. One-day passports give you unlimited access to rides and shows at either Disneyland or DisneySea. Opening hours for both vary seasonally, so phone ahead or check the website before you set out. Parking costs ¥2000 per day.

Shrine' and a memorial to Japan's victims of war. No wonder it invites controversy. Politics aside, it has a beautiful, contemplative inner sanctum in the style of ancient Ise shrines – a stark contrast to the *uyoku* (right-wing activists) shouting their rhetoric outside.

🛍 SHOP

North of the Marunouchi business district is the Kanda neighbourhood, which holds little of interest to travellers other than for bookworms. Jimbōchō is famous for its bookshops, serving all sorts of special-interest readers, from manga maniacs to collectors of antique maps. Northeast of Jimbōchō across the Kanda River is even more manga, and electronics, in Akihabara (Electric Town). But the most famous shopping mecca in Central Tokyo is glittery Ginza, its snob value still holding sway.

🎴 AKIHABARA GACHAPON KAIKAN 秋葉原 *Toys*
☎ 5209-6020; www.akibagacha.com; 1F, MN Bldg, 3-15-5 Soto-Kanda, Chiyoda-ku; ⏰ 11am-8pm; 🚃 JR Yamanote line to Akihabara (west exit)
Come with pockets full of 100-yen coins, as this shop houses hundreds of *gachapon* (capsule-vending machines) dispensing manga character toys, keychain and mobile-phone mascots and some-assembly-required figurines – perfect, pre-packaged Tokyo souvenirs.

🎴 HAIBARA はいばら
Stationery
☎ 3272 3801; 2-7-6 Nihombashi, Chūō-ku; ⏰ 9.30am-6.30pm Mon-Fri, 9.30am-5pm Sat; 🚇 Ginza, Tōzai, Toei Asakusa lines to Nihombashi (exits B8 & C3)
Even Haibara's business cards are made from exquisite paper. Find high-quality *washi* and tiny treasures such as wallets, hand mirrors and mobile-phone accessories

Naoya Suzuki
Rock-climbing guide & owner of Adventure Seekers (p63)

How long have you been a climber? In 2009, 16 years. **And a guide?** I became a certified climbing guide through the AMGA (American Mountain Guide Association) in 2003. **Where do you climb in Tokyo?** My favourite climbing gym is in Edogawa-bashi, but I don't like spending time and money at a gym. **Is it possible to do climbing day trips from Tokyo?** Absolutely. You could even go as far as Nagano if you take a car. Nearby, the climbing area at Mt Takao is only 20 minutes by bus, and there's tons of great hiking. Yugawara, in Kanagawa Prefecture, has *onsen* (hot springs), climbing, hiking…and there's Jogasaki, in Shizuoka Prefecture, with sea-cliff climbing and a 10km flat hiking trail, *onsen*, sushi. Super beautiful. **What's a good urban adventure within Tokyo?** Spend a day walking from Tsukiji to Roppongi without taking trains or taxis. Then have a beer!

made from printed paper in this jewellery box of a paper shop.

🏠 HAKUHINKAN TOY PARK
博品館 *Toys*

☎ 3571 8008; www.hakuhinkan.co.jp; 8-8-11 Ginza, Chūō-ku; ⏰ 11am-8pm; 🚇 JR Yamanote line to Shimbashi (Ginza exit), 🚇 Ginza & Toei Asakusa lines to Shimbashi (exits 1 & 3)

One of Tokyo's most famous toy stores, this 'toy park' is crammed to the rafters with dolls, action figures, squawking video games, seas of colourful plastic and the softest plush toys ever. Hakuhinkan also harbours child-friendly restaurants and even a theatre in this huge children's attention-deficit paradise.

🏠 HASHI GINZA NATSUNO
箸銀座夏野 *Handicrafts*

☎ 3569 0952; www.e-ohashi.com in Japanese; 1F & 6F, Ginza Takahashi Bldg, 6-7-4 Ginza, Chūō-ku; ⏰ 10am-8pm Mon-Sat, 10am-7pm Sun; 🚇 Ginza, Hibiya & Marunouchi lines to Ginza (exit B3)

Look out for this narrow shopfront in Ginza if you'd like to add some *hashi* (chopsticks) to your stash of souvenirs. Ginza Natsuno stocks a staggering array of *hashi*, from inexpensive, colourful children's sets to hand-carved pairs costing thousands of yen. Lovely chopstick rests, ceramics and decorations fill out every other corner of usable space.

🏠 ITŌYA 伊東屋 *Stationery*

☎ 3561 8311; 2-7-15 Ginza, Chūō-ku; ⏰ 9.30am-7pm Mon-Sat, 9.30am-6pm Sun; 🚇 Ginza, Hibiya & Marunouchi lines to Ginza (exits A12 & A13)

Nine floors of stationery-shop love await paper (and paperclip) fanatics at Itōya. In addition to a comprehensive collection of *washi*, there are Italian leather agendas, erasable pens in the season's coolest hues and even *tenugui* – beautifully hand-dyed, all-purpose traditional handkerchiefs.

COLD BREWS & WARM BREEZES

During the summer many large department stores open up rooftop beer gardens. While not actual gardens, they're great, casual places to hoist a few beers outdoors with the salarymen knocking off work early. There's usually a good assortment of European and Japanese pub-style food on the menu, and many places offer *tabehōdai* (all-you-can-eat) and *nomihōdai* (all-you-can-drink) deals for around ¥2500 (with a two-hour limit, usually). Check out the rooftops of Takashimaya (p57) in Nihombashi, Matsuya (right) in Ginza, or the pleasant gardenlike setting of **Kudan Kaikan** (☎ 3261 5521; 1-6-5 Kudan-Minami, Chiyoda-ku; ⏰ 5-10pm; 🚇 Hanzōmon, Tōzai & Toei Shinjuku lines to Kudanshita, exit 4).

CHOPSTICK TIPS

Although foreigners will be forgiven most dining faux pas, remember this basic *hashi* (chopstick) etiquette.

> As anywhere in Asia, never leave chopsticks upright in your rice bowl; this is only done at funerals.
> Don't pass food from one set of chopsticks to another, as this is associated with another funereal ritual.
> Use the other end of your chopsticks when picking up food from a shared plate, so as not to use the ends that go in your mouth.
> It's considered rude to gesture with or point at anyone with chopsticks; when you're not using them to eat, it's best to lay them on the table in front of you.
> If you must resort to stabbing your food rather than picking it up with your chopsticks, consider requesting a fork and knife.

🏠 LAOX ラオックス
Cameras & electronics

☎ 3253 7111; 1-2-9 Soto-Kanda, Chiyoda-ku; ⏰ 10am-9pm, closing hours vary at end of month; 🚇 JR Sōbu & Yamanote lines to Akihabara (Electric Town exit)

The multilingual staff at this duty-free Laox will help you figure out whether the voltage on your new superjuicer is compatible with your home voltage before you lug it on the plane. This huge chain, selling discounted electrical equipment, has very competitive prices. There's another duty-free Laox nearby.

🏠 MARUZEN 丸善 *Books*

☎ 5288 8881; 1F-4F, Oazo Bldg, 1-6-4 Marunouchi, Chiyoda-ku; ⏰ 9am-9pm; 🚇 JR Yamanote line to Tokyo (Marunouchi north exit)

Based in the curvy Oazo Building just across from Tokyo Station's Marunouchi exit, Maruzen boasts a satisfyingly wide selection of English-language books and magazines. The 4th floor is where you'll find the foreign-language material, a stationery shop and a café. Maruzen's original branch, accessible via exit B3 at Nihombashi Station, has foreign-language books on the 3rd floor.

🏠 MATSUYA 松屋
Department store

☎ 3567 1211; 3-6-1 Ginza, Chūō-ku; ⏰ 10.30am-7.30pm; 🚇 Ginza, Hibiya, Marunouchi lines to Ginza (exits A12 & A13)

A boon for foreign visitors, Matsuya offers the works with packaging and international shipping service, tax-exemption assistance and useful, if haphazard, in-store English-speaking guides. Don't forget to

NEIGHBOURHOODS

CENTRAL TOKYO

take a peek at Matsuya's art gallery on the 7th floor, and in the summer, the rooftop beer garden.

🛍 MIKIMOTO PEARL ミキモト真珠
Jewellery & accessories
☎ 3535 4611; www.mikimoto.com/jp/; 4-5-5 Ginza, Chūō-ku; ⏱ 11am-7pm; Ⓜ Ginza, Hibiya & Marunouchi lines to Ginza (exit B5)

Founded in 1899, Mikimoto Pearl was founded by the self-made Mikimoto Kokichi. At an early age he became fascinated with pearl divers and later developed the cultured pearl, building Mikimoto into the most famous of Tokyo's pearl shops. The store is located right next door to Wakō department store in Ginza.

🛍 MITSUKOSHI 三越
Department stores
☎ 3562 1111; 4-6-16 Ginza, Chūō-ku; ⏱ 10am-8pm, closed occasional Mon; Ⓜ Ginza, Hibiya, Marunouchi lines to Ginza (exits A7 & A11)

Tokyo's oldest department store was originally modelled on that London bastion of commerce, Harrods. Mitsukoshi is a posh and polished leviathan filled to the gills with tempting wares. Look for the Mitsukoshi lion at the corner entrance, which is a popular meeting spot for locals. There's also the original store in Nihombashi.

🛍 MUJI 無印良品
Clothing & homewares
☎ 5208 8241; 2F & 3F, 3-8-3 Marunouchi, Chiyoda-ku; ⏱ 10am-9pm; Ⓡ JR Yamanote line to Yūrakuchō (main exit), Ⓜ Yūrakuchō line to Yūrakuchō (exit A4b)

Mujirushi Ryōhin – literally, 'no-name brand' – is the paradoxical designer label that took Japan, then Paris, London and Hong Kong by storm. Everything is reasonably priced and simply designed, from tea sets to toddler clothing and travel gear. This is the flagship store, but you'll find other branches all over Tokyo.

🛍 OHYA SHOBŌ 大屋書房
Books
☎ 3291 0062; www.ohya-shobo.com; 1-1 Kanda Jimbōchō, Chiyoda-ku; ⏱ 10am-6pm Mon-Sat; Ⓜ Hanzōmon, Toei Mita & Toei Shinjuku lines to Jimbōchō (exit A7)

You could lose yourself for hours in this splendid, musty old bookshop specialising in ukiyo-e ('floating world' prints) and ancient maps. The friendly staff can help you find whatever particular piece of antiquated trivia your heart desires.

🛍 SOFMAP ソフマップ
Cameras & electronics
☎ 3253 1111; 4-1-1 Soto-Kanda, Chiyoda-ku; ⏱ 11am-9pm; Ⓡ JR Sōbu & Yamanote lines to Akihabara (Electric Town exit)

Crafty marketing, ruthless discounting and a staff of tech geeks have helped Sofmap sprout more than a dozen branches within Akihabara alone. The gigantic main shop has seven floors of electronics of all types, games, and new and used PCs, and is as overwhelmingly cacophonous as you would expect.

TAKASHIMAYA 高島屋
Department stores
☎ 3211 4111; 2-4-1 Nihombashi, Chūo-ku; 🕙 10am-7.30pm; ⓜ Ginza, Tōzai, Toei Asakusa lines to Nihombashi (exit B1 & B2)
In Nihombashi Takashimaya is one of the more venerable old establishments with palatial architecture. Primly dressed, white-gloved attendants operate the old-fashioned lifts and bow demurely as you arrive and depart; take the lift to the rooftop patio, where you can bring your *bentō* (boxed meal). There's another branch in Ginza and the enormous Takashimaya Times Square complex in Shinjuku.

TAKUMI HANDICRAFTS
たくみ *Handicrafts*
☎ 3571 2017; www.ginza-takumi.co.jp in Japanese; 8-4-2 Ginza, Chūo-ku; 🕙 11am-7pm Mon-Sat; ⓜ JR Yamanote line to Shimbashi (Ginza exit)
Takumi carries an elegant selection of toys, textiles, ceramics and other traditional folk crafts from around Japan. The shop also thoughtfully encloses information detailing the origin and background of any pieces you purchase.

TORA-NO-ANA
とらのあな *Books*
☎ 5294 0123; www.toranoana.co.jp; 4-3-1 Soto-Kanda, Chiyoda-ku; 🕙 10am 10pm; ⓡ JR Sōbu & Yamanote lines to Akihabara (Electric Town exit)
Keep your eyes up and look for the cute illustrated tiger-girl on

DOING THE DEPACHIKA

Tokyo's department stores are marvels unto themselves, not least because in their underground levels *depachika* (basement food halls) rule. Sure, there's the high-end grocery aspect to it, and the takeaway that takes your breath away – but they are an epicure's wet dream. This is where discriminating OLs (office ladies) and *obāsan* (grannies) purchase those archetypical hundred-dollar gift melons, the highest-grade, first-harvest tea and hand-rolled, bittersweet, Belgian-style truffles. Gourmet gifts abound, as well as sit-down counters where you can lunch on tempura or take away some *onigiri* (rice balls) for a picnic in the park. They're like every other Asian market in the world, except you could eat your *bentō* (boxed meal) off the immaculate floor – though, to be polite, we don't recommend it.

the top of this building, which has seven floors of manga and *anime*. Tora no Ana has other branches in Shinjuku and Ikebukuro.

🛍 UNIQLO ユニクロ *Fashion*
☎ 3569 6781; 5-7-7 Ginza, Chūō-ku; ⏰ 11am-9pm; Ⓜ Ginza, Hibiya & Marunouchi lines to Ginza (exit A2 & A3)
Like Muji and the Gap, Uniqlo has made a name for itself by sticking to the basics. Offering inexpensive clothing with simple lines, this chain has opened over 80 stores in Tokyo. A convenient place to pop in for an extra set of cheap jeans or plain shirts.

🛍 YODOBASHI AKIBA ヨドバシアキバ
Cameras & electronics
☎ 5209 1010; 1-1 Kanda-Hanaokachō, Chiyoda-ku; ⏰ 9.30am-10pm; 🚆 JR Sōbu & Yamanote lines to Akihabara (Electric Town exit)
This megalith of a discount store is located on the east side of Akihabara Station, with a whopping nine floors of cameras, computer equipment and enough electronics for the most hardcore geek.

🍴 EAT
Ginza is a great place to splash out on a quality Japanese dinner, at one of its classic establishments. For lunch there are heaps of excellent traditional *soba* (buckwheat

noodle) shops around less-pretentious Kanda, while the must-do sushi breakfast should be taken in Tsukiji, naturally.

For *yakitori* (skewers of grilled chicken) in the most atmospheric spot in the neighbourhood, try Yūrakuchō Yakitori Alley, a conglomeration of simple *yakitori* stalls beneath the JR tracks just south of Yūrakuchō station. It's noisy, smoky and convivial; sit yourself down and wash down your *yakitori* with some cold beer.

🍽 BIRDLAND バードラン
Yakitori   ¥¥
☎ 5250 1081; B1F, Tsukamoto Sozan Bldg, 4-2-15 Ginza, Chūō-ku; ⏰ 5-9pm Tue-Sat; Ⓜ Ginza, Hibiya & Marunouchi lines to Ginza (exits C6 & C8)
Who knew Gewürztraminer went so well with skewered chicken hearts? Birdland does. Before said hearts are set aflame, they belong to free-range chickens so pure that they can be ordered as sashimi. Upscale and in demand, Birdland limits your dinner to two hours and only takes same-day reservations (from noon) for its famous *yakitori*.

🍽 BOTAN ぼたん
Traditional Japanese   ¥¥¥
☎ 3251 0577; 1-15 Kanda-Sudachō, Chiyoda-ku; ⏰ 11.30am-8pm Mon-Sat; Ⓜ Marunouchi line to Awajichō (exits A3 & A5) or Toei Shinjuku line to Ogawamachi (exits A3 & A5); ♿

Botan has been making flawless *torisuki*, an Edo-period pot-stew, in the same buttonmaker's house for more than 100 years. Savouring a meal here will be a culinary highlight of a visit to Tokyo. Reservations are recommended.

🍴 DAIWA SUSHI 大和寿司
Sushi & sashimi　　　　　¥¥
☎ 3547 6807; 5-2-1 Tsukiji, Chūo-ku; 🕙 5am-1.30pm Mon-Sat, closed 2nd Wed of the month; 🚇 Toei Ōedo line to Tsukiji-shijō (exit A2); ♿ V ♿

Lines are unavoidable at Tsukiji's famed sushi bar, but once your first piece of sushi hits the counter gratification is inevitable. The sushi sets are a good bet if you're not comfortable ordering in Japanese, and though they'll be too polite to say so, you're expected to eat without wasting time and then give up your seat.

🍴 EDOGIN 江戸銀
Sushi & sashimi　　　　　¥¥¥
☎ 3543 4401; 4-5-1 Tsukiji, Chūo-ku; 🕙 11am-9.30pm Mon-Sat; 🚇 Hibiya line to Tsukiji (exit 2); ♿ V ♿

Reeling them in to the alleys northwest of Tsukiji Market with its fresh, oversized, but reasonably priced Edo-style sushi, Edogin has a functional feel that showcases its quality fish. At dinnertime it's worth shelling out for the *toku-jōnigiri* sushi set. There's no

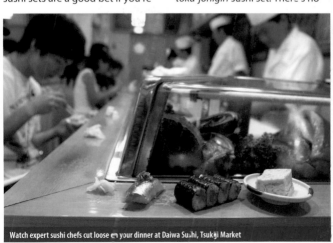

Watch expert sushi chefs cut loose on your dinner at Daiwa Sushi, Tsukiji Market

English sign outside, but it's easily identified by the plastic sushi in the window.

🍴 KANDA YABU SOBA
神田やぶそば
Soba ¥

☎ 3251 0287; 2-10 Kanda-Awajichō, Chiyoda-ku; ⏱ 11.30am-8pm; 🚇 Marunouchi line to Awajichō (exits A3 & A5) or Toei Shinjuku line to Ogawamachi (exits A3 & A5); ♿

A Kanda stalwart, this restaurant's authentic surroundings and sung-out orders heighten the experience. Yet, fittingly, it's the smooth *soba* (buckwheat noodles) that make the day. Look for queues of customers in front of the traditional Japanese building, its small garden surrounded by a wooden fence.

🍴 KYŪBEI 久兵衛
Sushi & sashimi ¥¥¥¥

☎ 3571 6523; 8-7-6 Ginza, Chūō-ku; ⏱ 11.30am-2pm & 5-10pm Mon-Sat; 🚆 JR Yamanote line to Shimbashi (Ginza exit), 🚇 Ginza line to Shimbashi (exits 1 & 2)

It's not just high-end fish you're paying for at Kyūbei, but the wonderful surroundings in a sushi restaurant widely considered to be one of Tokyo's best. Discreet to the point of being almost impossible to find, look for the minimalist Japanese façade with a small path

leading to the left. It's one street west of Chūō-dori.

🍴 L'OSIER
レストランロオジェ
French ¥¥¥¥

☎ 3571 6050; www.shiseido.co.jp/e/losier/top.htm; 7-5-5 Ginza, Chūō-ku; ⏱ noon-2.30pm & 6-9.30pm Mon-Sat; 🚇 Ginza, Hibiya & Marunouchi lines to Ginza (exit B6); ♿

Add to your extravagant expenditures in Ginza by reserving a table well in advance at L'Osier, which received a coveted three Michelin stars in 2008. The modern interpretations of classic French cuisine are exquisite and complemented by an imposing wine list. And if dinner seems too rich for your blood, lunch is a superb deal.

🍴 MATSUYA まつや
Soba ¥

☎ 3251 1556; 1-13 Kanda-Sudachō, Chiyoda-ku; ⏱ 11am-8pm; 🚇 Marunouchi line to Awajichō (exits A3 & A5) or Toei Shinjuku line to Ogawamachi (exits A3 & A5)

Rival to Kanda Yabu Soba and located almost next door, Matsuya is just as bustling and feels a notch more casual. Try plain *zaru soba*, then follow it up with the *kamo nanban, soba* with slices of roast duck. Soak it all up along with the merry crowd.

🍴 **MEIDI-YA** 明治屋
International groceries

☎ 3271 1134; 2-2-8 Kyōbashi, Chūō-ku; ⏰ 10am-8pm Mon-Sat, 11am-7pm Sun; ⊚ Ginza line to Kyōbashi (exit 7)

Meidi-ya specialises in high-end groceries for foreign palates, carrying cheeses, wines, cookies and other titbits you might crave in this foreign land. Note, there are other locations throughout the city, including branches in Akasaka and Ginza.

🍴 **MIMIU** 美々卯
Udon
¥¥

☎ 3567 6571; www.mimiu.co.jp; 3-6-4 Kyōbashi, Chūō-ku; ⏰ 11.30am-9.30pm Mon-Sat, 11.30am-9pm Sun; ⊚ Ginza line to Kyōbashi (exits 1 & 2)

This Osaka-based establishment has been turning out its famously silky *udon* since 1958. If you want to know what all the *udon* fuss is about, come to the stately black Kyōbashi branch for the *udon-suki* – perfect noodles nestle in a delicate bonito broth topped with seasonal vegetables, grilled meat and *yuba* (tofu skin).

🍴 **ROBATA** 爐端
Izakaya
¥¥

☎ 3591 1905; 1-3-8 Yūrakuchō, Chiyoda-ku; ⏰ 5-11pm Mon-Sat; ⊚ Hibiya & Chiyoda lines to Hibiya (exit A4)

Back near the railway tracks this is one of Tokyo's most celebrated *izakaya* (Japanese-style pub). A little Japanese language ability is helpful here, but the point-and-eat method works just fine. It's hard to spot the sign, even if you can read Japanese; better to look for the rustic, weathered façade.

🍴 **TEN-ICHI** 天一
Tempura
¥¥¥

☎ 3571 1949; 6-6-5 Ginza, Chūō-ku; ⏰ 11.30am-9.30pm; ⊚ Ginza, Hibiya, Marunouchi lines to Ginza (exits A1, B3 & B6)

One of Tokyo's oldest and best tempura restaurants, the refined and gracious Ten-Ichi is where one should go to experience tempura the way it's meant to be: light, airy and crispy. You'll find several branches elsewhere in Tokyo, but the distinguished Ginza original is the smartest. Reservations are recommended.

🍴 **YONEHANA** 米花
Traditional Japanese
¥¥

☎ 3541 4670; 5-2-1 Tsukiji, Chūō-ku; ⏰ 5am-1pm; ⊚ Toei Ōedo line to Tsukiji-Shijō (exits 1 & 2)

This family-run *unagi* (eel) restaurant in Tsukiji Market is now in the hands of its third generation, and the friendly, English-speaking chef is happy to make recommendations. It's an excellent spot to try *unagi* if you're not up for a sushi breakfast.

NEIGHBOURHOODS

CENTRAL TOKYO

🍸 DRINK

🍸 300 BAR *Bar*

☎ 3571 8300; www.300bar-8chome.com in Japanese; B1F, No 2 Column Bldg, 8-3-12 Ginza Chūō-ku; ⏱ 5pm-2am Mon-Sat, 5-11pm Sun; 🚃 JR Yamanote line to Shimbashi (Ginza exit)

One of the few places in Ginza that can truthfully say it offers a bargain, the 300 Bar charges ¥300 for everything – cocktails, snacks and all. There's no cover, and it's a fun place to stand around with a few drinks after some Ginza window-shopping.

🍸 AUX AMIS DES VINS
オザミデヴァン／ *Bar*

☎ 3567 4120; www.auxamis.com/desvins in Japanese; 2-5-6 Ginza, Chūō-ku; ⏱ 5.30pm-2am Mon-Fri & noon-midnight Sat; 🚇 Yūrakuchō line to Ginza-itchōme (exits 5 & 8)

Both the informal indoor and a small outdoor seating area at this wine bar feel welcoming in all seasons. A solid selection of mostly French wines comes by the glass (¥800) or by the bottle. You can also order snacks to go with your wine, or full prix-fixe dinners; lunch is served only on weekdays.

🍸 TAKARA 宝 *Izakaya*

☎ 5223 9888; B1F, Tokyo International Forum, 3-5-1 Marunouchi, Chiyoda-ku; ⏱ 11.30am-2.30pm & 5-11pm Mon-Fri, 11.30am-2.30pm & 5-10pm Sat & Sun; 🚃 JR Yamanote line to Yūrakuchō (main exit), 🚇 Yūrakuchō line to Yūrakuchō (exit A4b)

Those seeking to sample some sake should do themselves a favour and wander on into Takara, which has a dizzying sake selection and an English *izakaya* menu. This is a wonderfully unpretentious and classy spot for a sip.

MAID CAFÉS

Where *cosplay* (costume-play) culture and *otaku* (geeks; see p123) intersect, Akihabara would seem the obvious crux. This collision of subcultures results in a new iteration of an old game, with Tokyo's uniquely modern twist: maid cafés. This is master-slave role-playing as above-board commercial service, where young waitresses dressed in cartoonish French maid outfits serve the Akiba geeks who love them. Variations on the theme abound, with cafés employing women in drag playing slender, spiky-haired *anime* heroes, and even nun(!) cafés for those with Catholic fetishes. Look out for flyers and costumed touts, luring customers to the dozens of maid cafés that have set up shop in Akihabara.

PLAY

⭐ ADVENTURE SEEKERS
アドベンチャーシーカーズ
Rock climbing

☎ 050 1043 4287; www.adventure
-seekers.com; 152 Yaraichō, Shinjuku-ku,
Kindai-Hights 303; classes from ¥9000;
🕐 9am-6pm; Ⓜ Tōzai line to Kagurazaka (exit 1)

If Tokyo's urban wilderness has
you climbing the walls, the friendly, bilingual guides at Adventure
Seekers can get you out of the city
and onto a rock face. Private and
group classes are available with
professional and safety-oriented
guides, and they also offer a
variety of day trips to gorgeous
climbing escapes from Tokyo.

⭐ KABUKI-ZA 歌舞伎座
Theatre

☎ 3541 3131; www.shochiku.co.jp/play
/kabukiza/theater/index.html; 4-12-5
Ginza, Chūō-ku; admission ¥2500-17,000;
🕐 11am-9pm; Ⓜ Hibiya & Toei Asakusa
lines to Higashi-Ginza (exit 3)

Originally opened in 1889, Kabuki-
za has been rebuilt several times
following the Great Kantō Earthquake in 1923 and WWII bombing
in 1951. These days, its dramatic
and imposing architecture pops
out amid the modern edifices of
Higashi-Ginza, worth a walk-by
even if you don't plan on attend-
ing a performance…but take a
look before April 2010, when the
building and its beautiful façade
will be demolished for yet
another rebuild.

⭐ NATIONAL FILM CENTRE
フィルムセンター   *Cinema*

☎ 5777 8600; 3-7-6 Kyōbashi, Chūō-ku;
cinema ¥500/300/100, gallery ¥200/70/40;
🕐 cinema 3-10pm Tue-Fri, 1-7pm Sat
& Sun, gallery 11am-6.30pm Tue-Sat;
Ⓜ Ginza line to Kyōbashi (exit 2) or Toei
Asakusa line to Takarachō (exit A3)

The third arm of the National
Museum of Modern Art (p50), this
centre shows tremendous film
series on a range of subjects,
from the history of Japanese
animation to the masterpieces of
Cuba's film tradition. The centre
also houses a library and a gallery that includes a permanent
collection of antique cinematic
equipment.

⭐ NATIONAL THEATRE
国立劇場 *Theatre*

☎ 3230 3000; www.ntj.jac.go.jp/english
/index.html; 4-1 Hayabusachō, Chiyoda-ku;
admission ¥1500-12,000; 🕐 reservations 10am-6pm, performances 11.30am
& 5pm; Ⓜ Namboku & Yūrakuchō lines to
Nagatachō (exit 4)

Otherwise known as Kokuritsu
Gekijō, this theatre features

CENTRAL TOKYO

WORTH THE TRIP

On the east bank of the Sumida River, Ryōgoku is akin to a sumō village. Because the sumō stadium is located here, so too are the sumō *beya* (wrestling stables) that train and house *rikishi* (wrestlers).

During Grand Tournament time at **Ryōgoku Kokugikan** (☎ 3622 1100; www.sumo .or.jp; 1-3-28 Yokoami, Sumida-ku; ☯ 10am-4pm; ☒ JR Sōbu line to Ryōgoku (west exit), ☺ Toei Ōedo line to Ryōgoku (exit A4)), nonreserved seats in back sell for as little as ¥1500 and standing-room-only tickets are a meagre ¥500. Simply turn up on the day you'd like to attend, but get there early as keen punters start queuing the night before. Only one ticket is sold per person to foil scalpers, so come with your entire entourage.

When tournaments aren't in season, you can pick up a handbook at the stadium and take a self-guided walking tour of the neighbourhood and some of the local *beya*. Be sure to also take a peek into the **Sumō Museum** (☎ 3622 0366; www.sumo.or.jp/eng/museum/index

astonishingly lifelike, bunraku puppets, which are half to two-thirds life-size and each operated by three hooded, visible puppeteers. A single narrator, standing on a dais to one side, intones the story using a different voice for each character. Performances take place in Tokyo in February, May, September and December.

⭐ SESSION HOUSE
セッションハウス *Theatre*
☎ 3266 0461; 158 Yaraichō, Shinjuku-ku; admission varies; ☯ performances 7pm; ☺ Tōzai line to Kagurazaka (exit 1)

Dance aficionados consider Session House one of the best traditional, folk and modern dance spaces in the city. The theatre seats only 100 people, ensuring an intimate feel for all performances. Exit right from Kagurazaka Station,

make a right into the first narrow alley, and turn left where it dead-ends. Session House will be a few metres on your right.

⭐ TOKYO DOME
東京ドーム *Spectator sports*
☎ 5800 9999; www.tokyo-dome.co.jp/e; 1-3-61 Kōraku, Bunkyō-ku; from ¥1000; ☒ Chūō, Sōbu lines to Suidobashi (west exit), ☺ Marunouchi & Namboku lines to Kōrakuen (Kōrakuen exit)

A trip to a Japanese ballpark is truly a cultural experience in baseball-mad Japan. Fans in matching *happi* (half-coats) perform synchronised cheers, and entire sections of the extremely well-mannered crowd often wind up singing in unison. Tokyo Dome is the home turf of Japan's most popular team, the Yomiuri Giants.

.html; 1F, 1-3-28 Yokoami, Sumida-ku; admission free; 🕙 10am-4.30pm Mon-Fri; 🚇 Sōbu line to Ryōgoku, west exit, 🚇 Toei Ōedo line to Ryōgoku, exit A4), located inside Ryōgoku Kokugikan. Although there's little English explanation, exhibits are visually interesting enough to be worth a look. Note that during tournaments, the museum is open only to ticket-holding attendees.

Just behind Ryōgoku Kokugikan is the super☆ **Edo-Tokyo Museum** (☎ 3626 9974; www.edo-tokyo-museum.or.jp; 1-4-1 Yokoami, Sumida-ku; admission ¥600/300-480/free; 🕙 9.30am-5.30pm Tue-Fri & Sun, 9.30am-7.30pm Sat; 🚇 JR Sōbu line to Ryōgoku, west exit, 🚇 Toei Ōedo line to Ryōgoku, exit A4). Offering a fascinating view into Edo-era life, this museum is highly accessible by wheelchair, fun for kids and even has volunteers who give free tours in English (and other languages). Call ahead to confirm availability of such tour guides.

For more information on Sumo see p10.

Home-run hype hits Tokyo Dome

☆ TOKYO TAKARAZUKA GEKIJŌ 東京宝塚劇場
Theatre

☎ 5251 2001; http://kageki.hankyu.co.jp /english; 1-1-3 Yūrakuchō, Chiyoda-ku; admission ¥3500-10,000 🕙 times vary; 🚇 Chiyoda, Hibiya & Toei Mita lines to Hibiya (exits A5 & A13)

Kabuki kicked women out of the tradition, but the ladies have taken the ball and run with it at the Takarazuka Revue, founded in 1913. The extensively trained, all-female cast puts on an equally grand – if drastically different – show. These musical productions tend toward the soap-operatic and attract a disproportionate percentage of swooning female fans.

>UENO

Ueno-kōen (Ueno Park), the preeminent attraction to this Shitamachi neighbourhood, is a feast of culture with its numerous museums, temples and shrines. While most people enter the park at the museum plaza, another pleasant way to see the park before museum-fatigue sets in is to start at the south end. From the Shinobazu exit of the Ueno JR station, cross the road and go up the stairs to the left of the Keisei Ueno station entrance, up to the small pavilion where the Takamori Saigō statue stands. From there, continue uphill to the temple complex before heading out, near the zoo, into the museum area.

Also near the south end of the park is Shinobazu-ike, a large pond where lotuses proliferate and where you can rent small **boats** (☎ 3828 9502; rowboats per hr ¥600, paddle boats 30min ¥600; ⏲ 9am-5pm Mar-Nov) for a serene stint on the water's surface. This pond also has its own temple, Benten-dō, on an island.

UENO

🅞 SEE
Benten-dō (Ueno) 1 B4
Kiyōmizu Kannon-dō 2 C4
National Museum of
    Western Art 3 C3
National Science
    Museum 4 C3
Shitamachi History
    Museum 5 C5

Tokyo Metropolitan
    Museum of Art 6 C3
Tokyo National Museum
    (Tokyo Kokuritsu
    Hakubutsukan) 7 C3
Tōshōgū 8 B3
Ueno Zoo 9 B3
Yayoi Museum &
    Takehisa Yumeji
    Museum 10 A3

🅞 SHOP
Ameyoko Arcade 11 C5

🍴 EAT
Echikatsu 12 B5
Hantei 13 A3
Izu-ei 14 C5
Sasa-no-Yuki 15 D1
Ueno Yabu Soba 16 C5

See Asakusa Map (p75)

👁 SEE

👁 BENTEN-DŌ 弁天堂

☎ 3821 4638; 2-1 Ueno-kōen, Taitō-ku; admission free; 🕑 9am-5pm; 🚉 JR Yamanote line to Ueno (Shinobazu exit)

Take a stroll down the causeway leading to the island on which Benten-dō stands. The temple is dedicated to Benzaiten, the Buddhist goddess of the arts, wisdom, the sea and the protector of children (she covers a lot of territory). More interesting than the temple itself is its location and the opportunity to see the birds and botany that thrive around the pond.

👁 KIYOMIZU KANNON-DŌ 清水観音堂

1-4 Ueno-kōen, Taitō-ku; admission free; 🕑 9am-5pm; 🚉 JR Yamanote line to Ueno (Shinobazu exit)

This red temple, up the path from the Takamori Saigō statue, was modelled after Kiyomizu-dera in Kyoto. During Ningyō-kuyō (p33), women wishing to conceive a child leave a doll here for Senjū Kannon (the 1000-armed goddess of mercy), and the accumulated dolls are ceremonially burnt each 25 September.

👁 NATIONAL MUSEUM OF WESTERN ART 国立西洋美術館

☎ 5777 8600; 7-7 Ueno-koen, Taitō-ku, admission ¥420/130/free; 🕑 9.30-5.30 Tue-Thu, Sat & Sun, 9.30am-8pm Fri ; 🚉 JR Yamanote line to Ueno (Park exit); ♿

It may seem odd coming all this way just to check out Rodin sculptures and Le Corbusier architecture, but the Museum of Western Art can be well worth a stop during its frequent visiting exhibits. Check local listings for what's on during your visit; there are often extra admission fees for special exhibitions.

👁 NATIONAL SCIENCE MUSEUM 国立科学博物館

☎ 3822 0111; www.kahaku.go.jp/english; 7-20 Ueno-kōen, Taitō-ku; admission ¥600/free, additional fee for special exhibitions; 🕑 9am-5pm Tue-Thu, Sat & Sun, 9am-8pm Fri; 🚉 JR Yamanote line to Ueno (Park exit); ♿ 🚼

Renovations in recent years have made this museum more user-friendly for foreigners, with interpretive English signage throughout. The interactive exhibits are great fun for kids, especially those that allow clambering. Between the dinosaur displays here and the animals at Ueno Zoo (p71), this is an excellent outing for children.

👁 SHITAMACHI HISTORY MUSEUM 下町風俗資料館

☎ 3823 7451; 2-1 Ueno-kōen, Taitō-ku; admission ¥300/100; 🕑 9.30am-4.30pm Tue-Sun; 🚉 JR Yamanote line to Ueno (Hirokōji exit); ♿ 🚼

Learn some games and try on clothes in the style of Edo's Shi-tamachi, the plebeian downtown quarter of old Tokyo. Hands-on or walk-in exhibits include a sweet shop, the home and business of a copper-boiler maker and a tene-ment house (don't forget to take off your shoes).

TOKYO METROPOLITAN MUSEUM OF ART
東京都美術館

☎ 3823 6921; www.tobikan.jp; 8-36 Ueno-kōen, Taitō-ku; admission varies; ⏰ 9am-5pm, closed 3rd Mon of each month; 🚃 JR Yamanote line to Ueno (Park exit); ♿

The Tokyo Met has several galler-ies that run temporary displays of contemporary Japanese art. Galleries feature all manner of Western-style art and Japa-nese-style works such as *sumi-e* (ink-brush painting) and ikebana. Apart from the main gallery, the rental galleries are curated by the artists and collectives who rent them, so exhibitions are a mixed bag.

TOKYO NATIONAL MUSEUM 東京国立博物館

☎ 3822 1111; www.tnm.jp; 13-9 Ueno-kōen, Taitō-ku; admission ¥600/400/free; ⏰ 9.30am-5pm Tue-Thu, Sat & Sun, 9.30am-8pm Fri; 🚃 JR Yamanote line to Ueno (Park exit); ♿

Armed to the teeth at Tokyo National Museum

This showcase of Japanese and Asian art and artefacts is the crown jewel of Ueno Park museums. Mull over your visit with a stroll in the peaceful Tokugawa Shōgun Cem-etery, located just behind the museum.

TŌSHŌGŪ 東照宮

☎ 3822 3455; 1-9 Ueno-kōen, Taitō-ku; admission ¥200; ⏰ 9am-4.30pm; 🚃 JR Yamanote line to Ueno (Shinobazu exit)

Established in 1627, this shrine has the distinction of being one of the few extant early Edo

Meiko Fujimura
Ichimatsu dollmaker whose dolls are sold at Yoshitoku (p79)

How did you come to be a dollmaker? As my grandfather was a dollmaker, and so was my father, I was born into a dollmaker's house. **What's the most rewarding aspect about making dolls in this day and age?** I feel that I'm bringing children into the world. In this way it differs from other arts. Both I and the customer refer to the dolls as 'him' or 'her' rather than 'it'. When dolls get dirty or old, there are doll hospitals to rehabilitate them. One never throws them away; there are proper doll cremation ceremonies at shrines. **How are you carrying on the tradition?** It's not only a process; it's a philosophy, really, a culture. It's like joyful playing! It's life or death. As with all Japanese crafts, it's crucial to hand down the tradition, as I received it from my father and he received it from his.

structures, having survived the Great Kantō Earthquake of 1923, WWII destruction and other historical disasters. The intricate decoration and the architecture of the shrine, typical to other Tōshōgū shrines throughout Japan, and the atypical copper lanterns lining the path, are well worth the price of admission.

UENO ZOO 上野動物園

☎ 3828 5171; 9-83 Ueno-kōen, Taitō-ku; admission ¥600/200/free; ⏰ 9.30am-5pm Tue-Sun; Ⓜ Chiyoda line to Nezu (south exit), Ⓡ JR Yamanote line to Ueno (Park exit);

Established in 1882, Ueno Zoo was the first of its kind in Japan. It makes a good detour if you're travelling with kids; otherwise, it can be safely dropped from a busy itinerary. Sadly, the zoo's last charming giant panda passed on

GOT GRUTT?

Museum-crawlers planning on visiting several museums during a Tokyo visit should grab a Grutt Pass (¥2000) at the Tokyo Tourist Information Center (p202). The pass is a book of tickets entitling the bearer to free or discounted entry to nearly 50 Tokyo museums and zoos. It's valid for two months after the first visit and is a fabulous deal as it pays for itself in a few visits. The Grutt Pass is also available at participating museums.

in April 2008, but lions and tigers and okapis await.

YAYOI MUSEUM & TAKEHISA YUMEJI MUSEUM 弥生美術館　竹久夢二美術館

☎ 3812 0012; www.yayoi-yumeji-museum.jp; 2-4-2 Yayoi, Bunkyō-ku; admission ¥800/700/400; ⏰ 10am-5pm Tue-Sun; Ⓜ Chiyoda line to Nezu (exit 1)

These two charming brick museums focus mostly on illustrations from popular art, books and other precursors to Japan's manga tradition. The work represents graphic art from the Meiji, Taishō and Shōwa periods, including some Japanese-style Art Deco illustrations.

SHOP

AMEYOKO ARCADE アメ横 Market

Ⓡ JR Yamanote line to Okachimachi (north exit) or Ueno (Hirokōji exit), Ⓜ Ginza line to Ueno-Hirokōji (exit A5) or Hibiya line to Naka-Okachimachi (exit A5)

Ameya-yokochō, or Ameyoko for short, is one of the only old-fashioned outdoor markets in Tokyo. It was famous as a post-WWII black market, and even now it retains that throwback feel, with merchants calling out to attract customers and open-air stalls displaying dried seafood, herbs and mushrooms. The Ameyoko Center

NEIGHBOURHOODS

UENO

Monster sales and shopping in Ameyoko Arcade (p71)

Build ng contains stalls that sell imported spices, produce and herbs from mainland Asia, and there are a few clothing and shoe bargains around the market area.

EAT

ECHIKATSU 江知勝
Sukiyaki ¥¥¥
☎ 3811 5293; 2-31-23 Yushima, Bunkyō-ku; ⏰ 5-9.30pm Mon-Sat, closed Sat in Aug; ⊖ Chiyoda line to Yushima (exit 5); ♿ ♨

Within the exquisite environs of a grand old Japanese house, take in the beautiful ambience with your sukiyaki (thinly sliced beef, vegetables and tofu cooked in broth at your table) and *shabu-shabu* (thinly sliced beef and vegetables cooked in broth and dipped in vinegar and citrus sauces). Many of the tatami rooms overlook small gardens. The staff doesn't speak English but will make a genuine effort to communicate; reservations are recommended.

HANTEI はん亭
Traditional Japanese ¥¥
☎ 3828 1440; 2-12-15 Nezu, Taitō-ku; ⏰ noon-2pm & 5-10pm Tue-Sat, noon-2pm & 4-9.30pm Sun; ⊖ Chiyoda line to Nezu (Shinobazu exit)
The procession of *kushiage* (deep-fried meat, fish and vegetables on skewers) comes to your table in groups of threes, as you dine in this lovely wooden-walled, traditional restaurant that was spared from WWII bombing. They'll keep the various dishes coming until you've had enough. Reservations (Japanese only) are recommended.

IZU-EI 伊豆栄
Traditional Japanese ¥¥
☎ 3831 0954; 2-12-22 Ueno, Taitō-ku; ⏰ 11am-9.30pm; ⊖ Chiyoda line to Yushima (exit 2), ⊜ JR Yamanote line to Ueno (Shinobazu exit)

Beautifully presented, authentic Japanese eel meals make this an excellent spot to take Japanese friends or colleagues to dinner. The Izu-ei *unagi bentō* (eel boxed dinner) includes tempura and is best eaten near the window for a lovely view of the giant lilypads on Shinobazu-ike. There's a limited picture menu.

ⅲ SASA-NO-YUKI 笹乃雪
Traditional Japanese ¥¥
☎ 3873 1145; 2-15-10 Negishi, Taitō-ku; www.sasanoyuki.com; ❍ 11am-8pm Tue-Sun; 🚇 JR Yamanote line to Uguisu-dani (north exit); Ⓥ 🛗
Sasa-no-Yuki, or 'snow on bamboo', opened in Edo over 300 years ago. Staying true to its roots, this establishment continues to serve tofu in dozens of forms and in *tōfu-ryōri* (multi-course, tofu-based meals). Strict

vegetarians should note that many dishes include chicken and fish stock; ask the friendly staff for advice if the English menu doesn't provide you with enough information.

ⅲ UENO YABU SOBA
上野やぶそば
Soba ¥
☎ 3831 4728; 6-9-16 Ueno, Taitō-ku; ❍ 11.30am-9pm Thu-Tue; 🚇 JR Yamanote line to Ueno (Hirokōji exit); 🛗
Near the arcade, this busy, famous place rustles up top-class *soba*, from the simple *zaru soba* – plain, cold buckwheat noodles to dip in broth – to the richly filling *tenseiro* (noodles topped with shrimp and vegetable tempura). There's a picture menu to help you choose. Look for the black-granite sign in front that says in English 'Since 1892'.

>ASAKUSA

While Asakusa does draw significant tourist traffic, it carries on with the rough-around-the-edges Shitamachi spirit that powered the low city of old Edo. With its bustling centrepiece the temple Sensō-ji drawing devotees as well as photo-snapping visitors, the streets, temples and shrines of Asakusa imbue this area with a historical feel. So too do the neighbourhood's working artists busily keep customs alive by labouring over traditional handicrafts.

The neighbourhood, with kitchenware district Kappabashi-dōri to the west and the Sumida River to the east, is compact enough to take in with a walking tour. But near Kaminarimon you'll probably also be wooed by *jinrikisha* (people-powered rickshaw) drivers in traditional dress, who can cart you around on tours (from ¥2100 per person for 10 minutes), stopping at sights to provide insightful commentary in English, Japanese or other languages. Asakusa runs at a steady hum throughout the day, but tends to shut down after night falls.

ASAKUSA

🅒 SEE
Asakusa-jinja 1 C2
Chingodō-ji (Chingodō
    Shrine) 2 B3
Dembō-in 3 B3
Edo Shitamachi
    Traditional Crafts
    Museum 4 B2
Sensō-ji 5 C2
Taiko-Kan
    (Drum Museum) 6 A3

🅒 SHOP
Kappabashi-Dōri 7 A3
Yoshitoku 8 A6

🍴 EAT
Daikokuya 9 B3
Irokawa 10 B4
Komagata Dōjō 11 B4
Sometarō 12 A3
Vin Chou 13 A3

🅈 DRINK
Asahi Sky Room 14 C4
Kamiya Bar 15 C4

⭐ PLAY
Asakusa Kannon
    Onsen 16 B2
Jakotsu-yu 17 B3

Imado 今戸

A · **B** · **C** · **D**

Kokusai-dōri

1

Kototoi-dōri

Sumida-kōen

Taitō-ku

Asakusa

2
Hikajo-dōri
Asakusa View Hotel

Hanayashiki Amusement Park
⊠16

Asakusa-kōen

Kototoi-dōri 言問通り

Kototoi-bashi

Umamichi-dōri
Hanakawadokōen

Kappabashihon-dōri

⊠ Asakusa

Dembō-in

Hōzō-mon

Hanakawado

Yoshino-dōri

Shuto Expwy No 6 首都高速6号

Nishi-Asakusa
西浅草

Asakusa Engei Hall

3
7 ⊠

13 ⊞
12 ⊞
6 ⊞

Tokyo Hongan-ji

Shin-Nakamise-dōri

17 ⊞

Kappabashi-dōri かっぱ橋通り

Orange-dōri オレンジ通り

2 ⊞
3 ⊞

Nakamise-dōri 仲見世通り

Tōbu Asakusa

Tōbu Asakusa

15 ⊞

Edo-dōri

Asakusa

Suijc Bus Pier

Asahi Super Dry Building

Asakusa 浅草

Kaminarimon-dōri

Chiyoda-dōri 千代田通り

Metro-dōri

Kaminarimon
雷門

Azumabashi 吾妻橋

14 ⊞

4
Tawaramachi

Asakusa-dōri

10 ⊞

Komagata-bashi 駒形橋

Honjo-Azumabashi

Kokusai-dōri 国際通り

11 ⊞

Kotobuki

Misume-dōri

5
Kasuga-dōri

Kuramae

Sumida River (Sumida-gawa) 隅田川

Shuto Expwy No 6 首都高速6号

6
Asakusabashi

8 ⊠

N
LP
0 · 200 m
0 · 0.1 miles

◉ SEE

◉ ASAKUSA-JINJA 浅草神社

2-3-1 Asakusa, Taitō-ku; admission free;
☎ Ginza & Toei Asakusa lines to Asakusa
(exits 1 & A5)

Buddhist Sensō-ji sits just in front of
its Shintō neighbour, Asakusa-jinja,
in silent architectural testament to
the peaceful coexistence of these
two religions in Japan. Also known
as Sanja-sama, this shrine is the site
of one of Tokyo's most important
matsuri (p31).

◉ CHINGODŌ-JI 鎮護寺

2-3-1 Asakusa, Taitō-ku; admission free;
☎ Ginza & Toei Asakusa lines to Asakusa
(exits 1 & A5)

This quiet, odd little shrine on the
banks of Dembō-in (right) pays
tribute to *tanuki* – the 'raccoon
dog' tricksters who figure in Japanese mythology. Shape-shifting
tanuki are normally depicted with
enormous testicles on which
they can fly.

◉ DEMBŌ-IN 伝法院

☎ 3842 0181; 2-3-1 Asakusa, Taitō-ku;
admission free; ⏰ 9am-4.30pm, closed
for ceremonies; ☎ Ginza & Toei Asakusa
lines to Asakusa (exits 1 & A5)

Adjacent to the Sensō-ji precinct
is Dembō-in, a temple with an at-
tached garden. Inside this secret
sanctuary there's a picturesque
pond and a replica of a famous
Kyoto teahouse. Although it's not
open to the public, you can make
an appointment to visit by calling
a few days ahead to the temple
office (inside the Five-Storeyed
Pagoda).

◉ EDO SHITAMACHI TRADITIONAL CRAFTS MUSEUM 江戸下町伝統工芸館

☎ 3842 1990; 2-22-13 Asakusa, Taitō-ku;
admission free; ⏰ 10am-8pm;
☎ Tsukuba Express to Asakusa (exit A1)
or Ginza line to Tawaramachi (exit 3)

This hall is a wonderful place to
view the handicrafts that continue

VISITING A SHRINE

Just past the *torii* (shrine gate) is a *chōzuya* (water trough), with long-handled ladles perched on
a rack above. This is for purifying yourself before entering the sacred precincts of the shrine. If
you choose to purify yourself, take a ladle, fill it with fresh water from the spigot, pour some over
one hand, transfer the spoon and pour water over the other hand. Then pour a little water into a
cupped hand and rinse your mouth, spitting the water onto the ground beside the trough.

Head to the *haiden* (hall of worship), which sits in front of the *honden* (main hall) enshrin-
ing the *kami* (shrine god). Toss a coin into the offerings box, ring the gong by pulling on the
thick rope in order to summon the deity, pray, then clap your hands twice, bow and then
back away from the shrine.

Sensō-ji Temple illuminates the sky at dusk

to flourish in Shitamachi. The gallery on the 2nd floor of this museum displays a rotating selection of works (such as fans, lanterns, knives, intricate woodcarvings and glass) by neighbourhood artists, and crafts demonstrations take place around noon on most weekends.

☉ SENSŌ-JI 浅草寺
☎ 3842 0181; 2-3-1 Asakusa, Taitō-ku; admission free; ☉ Ginza & Toei Asakusa lines to Asakusa (exits 1 & A5)

With its pagoda and shrines nearby, Sensō-ji is one of Tokyo's most popular sights. It lies in the heart of Asakusa and serves as a community temple. As you reach

Hōzōmon, the second gate leading into the temple itself, have a look at the Five-Storeyed Pagoda to the left, the second-tallest in Japan.

☉ TAIKOKAN (DRUM MUSEUM) 太鼓館
☎ 3842 5622; 2-1-1 Nishi-Asakusa, Taitō-ku; admission ¥300/150; ☽ 10am-5pm Wed-Sun; ☉ Ginza line to Tawaramachi (exit 3)

It's tellingly human that the vast majority of us can't resist the temptation to bang a gong, given half the chance. Luckily for our percussive tendencies, this drum museum makes its instruments fair game unless they're marked with a red dot. From *taiko* (traditional Japanese drums) to African finger-harps, this museum displays examples of drums from around the world.

🛍 SHOP

Nakamise-dōri, the lively pedestrian street leading to Sensō-ji, is chock-a-block with shops selling tourist wares like *geta* (wooden sandals worn with kimonos), lacquer combs, purses and cigarette cases made from kimono fabric and Edo-style toys and trinkets. Look out for stalls selling *sembei* (savoury rice crackers), *anko* (azuki-bean paste) sweets and freshly made *mochi* (sticky-rice cakes). But don't just stick to the main drag; the alleys off to both sides of Nakamise-dōri, and the streets around Sensō-ji are full of small shops selling *tenugui* (traditionally dyed hand towels) or accessories to be worn with kimonos and other fine handicrafts.

🛍 KAPPABASHI-DŌRI
かっぱ橋通り
Homewares & novelties

On the west side of Asakusa is this kitchenware shopping strip, which supplies restaurants and locals with items such as ceramic ware, woven bamboo trays, iron

These plastic food models go down a treat on Kappabashi-dōri, Asakusa's kitchenware shopping strip

teapots, *noren* (doorway curtains) and best of all, those excellent plastic food models. They don't come cheap though – a couple of pieces of sushi will set you back about ¥2500.

🏠 YOSHITOKU 吉徳
Specialist store

☎ 3863 4419; 1-9-14 Asakusabashi, Taitō-ku; ⏰ 9.30am-5.30pm Mon-Sat; 🚃 JR Sōbu line to Asakusabashi (main exit) 🚇 Toei Asakusa line to Asakusa-bashi (exit A2)

Dollmaker to the emperor, Yoshitoku has been in business since 1711. The dolls here are exquisitely crafted in silk and porcelain, dressed in sumptuous replicas of elaborate kimonos and accessories. Small pieces can sell for ¥2000, while more elaborate dolls can go for a hundred times as much. See also p70.

🍴 EAT

🍴 DAIKOKUYA 大黒家
Tempura ¥¥

☎ 3844 1111; 1-38-10 Asakusa, Taitō-ku; dishes ¥1500-3000; ⏰ 11.30am-8.30pm Mon-Fri, 11.30am-9pm Sat; 🚇 Ginza & Toei Asakusa lines to Asakusa (exits 1 & A5); ♿

Near Nakamise-dōri, this famous place serves great, authentic tempura, a speciality in Asakusa. The line out the door usually snakes around the corner at lunchtime,

but f it looks unbearably long, try your luck at the branch on the next block.

🍴 IROKAWA 色川 *Unagi* ¥¥

☎ 3844 1187; 2-6-11 Kaminarimon, Taitō-ku; ⏰ 11.20am-1.30pm & 5-8.30pm Mon-Sat; 🚇 Ginza & Toei Asakusa lines to Asakusa (exits 2 and A1)

Irokawa serves some of the best, most beautifully grilled *unagi* (eel) in Tokyo. Try the *unaju* (broiled eel on rice). It has a humble, traditional-looking exterior, with plants flanking the entrance, and is a friendly neighbourhood spot to try *unagi* with the locals.

🍴 KOMAGATA DOJŌ
駒形 どぜう
Dojō ¥¥

☎ 3842 4001; 1-7-12 Komagata, Taitō-ku; ⏰ 11am-9pm; 🚇 Ginza & Toei Asakusa lines to Asakusa (exits 2 & A5); ♿

The 6th-generation chef running this marvellous restaurant continues the tradition of elevating the simple *dojō* (a small, eel-like river fish) to a thing of delicious wonder. You can try it 10 different ways, and there's an English menu. Floor seating at the shared, low wooden plank tables heightens the traditional flavour, but ladies: don't wear a skirt for this dining expedition.

🍴 SOMETARŌ 染太郎
Okonomiyaki　　¥

☎ 3844 9502; www.sometaro.com in Japanese; 2-2-2 Nishi-Asakusa, Taitō-ku; ⏰ noon-10pm; ⓔ Ginza line to Tawaramachi (exit 3)

Inside the sliding door of this rustic-looking shop is the kind of friendly, traditional interior you'd expect, with a raised tatami floor and well-seasoned tabletop grills. The aroma filling the room comes from the *okonomiyaki*, a cook-it-yourself Japanese pancake you customise to your taste and grill at your table.

🍴 VIN CHOU 萬鳥
Yakitori　　¥¥

☎ 3845 4430; 2-2-13 Nishi-Asakusa, Taitō-ku; ⏰ 5pm-11pm Thu-Sat, Mon & Tue, 4-10pm Sun; ⓔ Ginza & Toei Asakusa lines to Asakusa (exits 1 & A5)

Tucked away in this corner of Asakusa, Vin Chou is an odd bird: a French-style *yakitori* joint, offering foie gras with your *tori negi* (chicken and spring onion). With cheeses and fowl imported from Europe, it's chic and unique. It's just round the corner one block west of the Taikokan (p77).

🍸 DRINK

Asakusa is another of those neighbourhoods without a compelling nightlife, but you can certainly throw back a few at these local bars.

🍸 ASAHI SKY ROOM
アサヒスカイルーム *Bar*

☎ 5608 5277; 22F, Asahi Super Dry Bldg, 1-23-1 Azumabashi, Sumida-ku; ⏰ 10am-10pm; ⓔ Ginza & Toei Asakusa lines to Asakusa (exits 4 & A5)

Spend the day at religious sites and end at the Asahi altar, on the 22nd floor of the golden-tinged Asahi Super Dry Building. Directly adjacent to the infamous *Flamme d'Or* sculpture (aka 'The Golden Turd') on the east bank of the Sumida River, the venue itself isn't noteworthy, but serves up Asahi brews and a spectacular view, especially at sunset.

🍸 KAMIYA BAR 神谷バー
Bar

☎ 3841 5400; 1-1-1 Asakusa, Taitō-ku; ⏰ 11.30am-10pm Wed-Mon; ⓔ Ginza & Toei Asakusa lines to Asakusa (exits 3 & A5)

Once popular with the Tokyo literati, this smoky old place hasn't changed much since it was founded in 1880. The 1st floor is a beer hall where you pay for drinks as you enter. Its best-known offering is the brandy-based cocktail *denki-bran*. The restaurants upstairs serve Japanese and Western food, but that's not the reason to come here.

⭐ PLAY

ASAKUSA KANNON ONSEN
浅草観音温泉 *Hot spring*
☎ 3844 4141; 2-7-26 Asakusa, Taitō-ku;
admission ¥700; 🕑 6.30am-6pm Thu-Tue;
Ⓖ Ginza & Toei Asakusa lines to Asakusa
(exits 1 & A5)

Look for the ivy-covered exterior
of this large, traditional bathhouse. The water here is a steamy
40°C, and Asakusa's historic ambience makes this a great place for
a soul-soothing soak.

⭐ JAKOTSU-YU 蛇骨湯
Hot spring
☎ 3841 8645; www.jakotsuyu.co.jp in
Japanese; 1-11-11 Asakusa, Taitō-ku;
admission ¥400; 🕑 1pm-midnight
Wed-Mon; Ⓖ Ginza line to Tawaramachi
(exit 3)

Jakotsu-yu is a wonderful little
neighbourhood *onsen* (hot
spring) with mineral-rich dark

TATTOO BLUES

Long the mark of the *yakuza* (mafia),
irezumi (tattoos) are still largely taboo
in Japan. Although body art is becoming more popular with younger people,
tattoos are still not as commonplace as
in the West. If your skin bears a tattoo or
a few, be discreet when visiting a *sentō*
(public bath) or *onsen* (hot spring). They
usually post signs prohibiting entry to
tattooed individuals, ostensibly to keep
out the *yakuza*. In reality, if the *yakuza*
want in, they'll get in – and in all like-
lihood you won't be mistaken for one.
Keep in mind, however, that your ink
may get you ejected.

water at a hot-hot-hot 45°C. This
onsen has a small *rotemburo*
(outdoor bath) with a garden
setting. From Kokusai-dōri, turn
into the second alley north of
Kaminarimon-dōri, then slip into
the first narrow alley on the right
and you're there.

>IKEBUKURO

Ikebukuro's former claim to fame was having Japan's hugest department stores, Asia's tallest building and the world's longest escalator. While those days are well and truly behind it, Ikebukuro's very unpretentiousness gives it a humble appeal, and there are some fabulous places to take kids. East Ikebukuro has also become a haven for the quietly burgeoning fringe population of *otome* (literally 'maidens'; colloquially 'girl geeks'), the female counterparts of their more famous brethren, the *otaku* ('geek boys'). Although these fangirls themselves are not as colourful as the *cosplay-zoku* (costume-play gangs), this fascinating subculture exemplifies Ikebukuro's less obvious cultural appeal.

Most of the entertainment is on the east side, where the small alleys contain karaoke bars, *pachinko* (pinball) parlours, a few maid cafés and love hotels. Follow Sunshine 60-dōri to Sunshine City. On the west side, have a look at the folk arts on display at the Japan Traditional Crafts Center or grab some cheap eats at a local *kaitenzushi* (conveyor-belt sushi bar) or *rāmen* (egg noodles) shop.

A
B
C
D

1

Shuto Expwy no 5 首都高速5号
☒ *Kita-ikebukuro*

200 m
0.1 miles

2

Ikebukuro
池袋

Gekijō-dōri

Kami-Ikebukuro
上池袋

Higashi-Ikebukuro
東池袋

Sakashita-dōri
Tokiwa-dōri

Bunka-dōri

Meiji-dōri 明治通り

Kasuga-dōri 春日通り

3

Azalea-dōri
13 🏨
M 🏨
Ⓜ *Ikebukuro*
Y 12

3 🏨
Ikebukuro
Mitsukoshi
4 🏨

Otome
Road

Otome-dōri

9 🏨
10 🏨
Nishi-Ikebukuro
kōen

Ikebukuro
Nishi-guchi-kōen
Metropolitan
Exit

Ⓜ *Ikebukuro*
2 🏨
1 Ⓞ

8 🏨

Metropolitan-
dōri メトロ通り

6 🏨
5 🏨
Fukutoshin

7 🏨 11 🏨
World Import
Mart Building

Nishi-Ikebukuro
西池袋

Seibu

Green-dōri

4

Minami-Ikebukuro kōen
南池袋公園

Shuto Expwy No 5 首都高速5号

Higashi-ikebukuro

Minami-Ikebukuro
南池袋

5

Satomi
Building

Meiji-dōri 明治通り

Tōshima-ku
豊島区

☒ *Zōshigaya*
(Streetcar Stop)

Zōshigaya Rei-en
(Zōshigaya Cemetery)
雑司が谷公園

🚃 *Mejiro*

Mejiro
目白

Mejiro-dōri

Mejiro-dōri 目白通り

Shimo-
Ochiai
落合

☒ *Zōshigaya*

☒ *Kishibojinmae*

Gakushein
University

SEE
SUNSHINE INTERNATIONAL AQUARIUM
サンシャイン国際水族館

☎ 3989 3466; 10F, World Import Mart Bldg, 3-1-3 Higashi-Ikebukuro, Toshima-ku; admission ¥1800/900; ☼ 10am-6pm; 🚆 JR Yamanote line to Ikebukuro (east exit); ♿ 🚻

Boasting the distinction of being the highest aquarium in the world, this high-rise water world has tanks full of electric eels, sharks and other intriguing sea life. Also living here are some incongruous land-lubbin' critters as well, like lemurs. The building is full of stimulating stuff for kids, such as a planetarium, shopping mall and food-themed amusement park.

SUNSHINE STARLIGHT DOME サンシャインスターライトドーム

☎ 3989 3475; 10F, World Import Mart Bldg, 3-1-3 Higashi-Ikebukuro, Toshima-ku; admission ¥800/500; ☼ noon-5.30pm Mon-Fri, 11am-6.30pm Sat & Sun; 🚆 JR Yamanote line to Ikebukuro (east exit); ♿ 🚻

We may be in down-to-earth Ikebukuro but some of us are looking at the stars. Alas, the planetarium's show is narrated in Japanese, but the visuals are spectacular enough to lift you out of this earthly end of Tokyo.

TOYOTA AMLUX
トヨタアムラックス

☎ 5391 5900; www.amlux.jp/english /access; 3-3-5 Higashi-Ikebukuro,

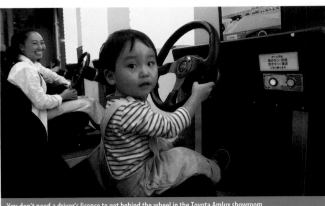
You don't need a driver's licence to get behind the wheel in the Toyota Amlux showroom

OTOME ROAD

'Maiden Road', as it's called, is like alternate-universe Akihabara for the *otome* (geek girls), the female equivalent of *otaku* (p123). Most *otome* – some of whom are actually grown women in their 40s – hang here at the local manga shops to browse 'boys' love' manga (exactly what it sounds like). They even have their own versions of role-play cafés featuring butlers instead of maids…with women in drag waiting tables as butlers.

Toshima-ku; admission free; ☺ 11am-7pm Tue-Sun; ☷ JR Yamanote line to Ikebukuro (east exit); ☷ ☷ Toyota's Auto Salon features concept cars and virtual-reality driving experiences, which are only two aspects of this fascinating showroom for the mechanically minded. It's a six-storey multi-media extravaganza, with short movies, aerodynamic architecture and visions of vehicular beauty everywhere. There's an English-language floor guide available.

SHOP

☐ BIC CAMERA
ビックカメラ
Cameras & electronics

☎ 5396 1111; 1-41-5 Higashi-Ikebukuro, Toshima-ku; ☺ 10am-9pm; ☷ JR Yamanote line to Ikebukuro (east exit)
Bic Camera may or may not be, as it claims, the cheapest camera store in Japan, but its ubiquity cannot be contested. Bic has other branches in Ikebukuro (☎ 3590 1111; 1-11-7 Higashi-Ikebukuro, Toshima-ku; ☺ 10am-9pm; ☷ JR Yamanote line to Ikebukuro (east exit)), as well as in Shibuya and Shinjuku. Deals are very competitive, but as always, shop around.

☐ BIC CAMERA (PC STORE)
Cameras & electronics

☎ 5956 1111; 1-6-7 Higashi-Ikebukuro, Toshima-ku; ☺ 10am-9pm; ☷ JR Yamanote line to Ikebukuro (east exit)
Another branch of Bic Camera specialising in PCs, in addition to many other branches all over Tokyo.

☐ JAPAN TRADITIONAL CRAFTS CENTER
全国伝統的工芸品センター
Handicrafts

☎ 5954 6066; www.kougei.or.jp/english /center html; 1F & 2F, Metropolitan Plaza Bldg, 1-11-1 Nishi-Ikebukuro, Toshima-ku; ☺ 11am-7pm; ☷ JR Yamanote line to Ikebukuro (Metropolitan exit)
Apart from being a wonderful place to find high-quality souvenirs such as weavings, regional ceramics, *washi* (handmade paper) and woodwork, this centre is a destination in its own right as a showcase for traditional crafts from all over Japan. Temporary exhibitions, demonstrations and classes are held on the 2nd floor.

🖾 LOFT ロフト
Homewares & novelties

☎ 5949 3880; 1-28-1 Minami-Ikebukuro, Toshima-ku; 🕙 10am-9pm Mon-Sat, 10am-8pm Sun; 🚇 JR Yamanote line to Ikebukuro (east exit)

Loft stocks all sorts of fun and sometimes functional homewares, stationery and gift items. It has another store in Shibuya (p122).

🖾 SUNSHINE CITY
サンシャインシティ
Department store

☎ 3989 3331; 3-1 Higashi-Ikebukuro, Toshima-ku; observation deck ¥620; 🕙 10am-10pm; 🚇 JR Yamanote line to Ikebukuro (east exit)

Billed as a 'city in a building', Sunshine City is another sprawling shopping centre, where for a small fee you can get catapulted in a speeding elevator to the 60th-floor observatory to peer out across the Tokyo skyline. If you're lucky, you might catch a glimpse of Mt Fuji beyond the haze.

🖾 TŌKYŪ HANDS
東急ハンズ
Homewares & novelties

☎ 3980 6111; 1-28-10 Higashi-Ikebukuro, Toshima-ku; 🕙 10am-9pm; 🚇 JR Yamanote line to Ikebukuro (east exit)

Not only does this branch of Tōkyū Hands sell all the fabulous booty for which it's famous, it also houses Nekobukuro (opposite).

Other stores can be found in Shinjuku (p94) and Shibuya (p124).

🍴 EAT

AKIYOSHI 秋吉 *Yakitori* ¥¥
☎ 3982 0644; 3-30-4 Nishi-Ikebukuro, Toshima-ku; 🕙 5-11pm; 🚇 JR Yamanote line to Ikebukuro (west exit); 🚼

Akiyoshi is the place to try for tasty *yakitori* (skewers of grilled chicken) in approachable, noisy and laid-back surroundings. This *yakitori* specialist certainly knows its stuff, while the picture menu is also a boon for non-Japanese speakers.

🍴 MALAYCHAN
マレーチャン *Malaysian* ¥
☎ 5391 7638; www.malaychan.jp/New Files/contents_E.html; 3-22-6 Nishi-Ikebukuro, Toshima-ku; 🕙 5-11pm Mon, 11am-2.30pm & 5-11pm Tue-Sat, 11am-11pm Sun; 🚇 JR Yamanote line to Ikebukuro (west exit); 🚼

With its great location on a corner across from Nishi-Ikebukuro Park, Malaychan is Ikebukuro's most pleasant place to eat. Its Malaysian cuisine is also a rarity in Tokyo, serving a tasty breadth of dishes representing the country's multiethnicity.

🍴 NAMCO NAMJATOWN
ナムコナンジャタウン
Food-themed park ¥
☎ 5950 0765; 2F & 3F, World Import Mart Bldg, 3-1-3 Higashi-Ikebukuro, Toshima-ku; admission ¥300/200;

🕙 10am-10pm; 🚉 JR Yamanote line to Ikebukuro (east exit)

Namco Namjatown houses three food-themed parks, specialising variously in *gyōza* (dumplings), cream puffs and ice cream. Is your mouth watering yet? Maybe it's just us. Admission fees only get you in; you pay for any goodies you eat.

🍸 DRINK

🍸 BOBBY'S BAR

ボビーズバー *Bar*

☎ 3980 8875; www.geocities.com/bobbys bartokyo/bobbys.html; 3F, 1-18-10 Nishi-Ikebukuro, Toshima-ku; 🕙 6pm-late Mon-Sat; 🚉 JR Yamanote line to Ikebukuro (west exit)

Sometimes a Tokyo visitor requires a break from the dazzling array of novel tastes and textures and instead needs to savour one's adventures of the day over a plate of fish and chips and a glass of Guinness. For such occasions, a drink at Bobby's hits the spot.

🍸 SASASHŪ 笹周 *Izakaya*

☎ 3971 6796; 2-2-6; Ikebukuro, Toshima-ku; 🕙 5-10pm Mon-Sat; Ⓜ Marunouchi line to Ikebukuro (exit C5); ♿

Serving delicacies such as *ka-monabe* (duck stew), Sasashū is a

DRINKING ETIQUETTE

When you're out for a few drinks, remember that you're expected to keep the drinks of your companions topped up. But don't fill your own glass, as this implies your guests aren't taking care of you; wait for someone to pour yours. It's polite to hold the glass with both hands while it's being filled. And most importantly, remember to say, '*Kampai!*' – cheers!

highly respected sake specialist maintaining a dignified old façade amid west Ikebukuro's strip joints. If you lack Japanese language ability, trust the master to guide your culinary experience by asking for *omakase* (chef's choice).

⭐ PLAY

⭐ NEKOBUKURO

ねこぶくろ *Petting zoo*

☎ 3980 6111; 8F, Tōkyū Hands, 1-28-10 Higashi-Ikebukuro, Toshima-ku; admiss on ¥600; 🕙 10am-8pm; 🚉 JR Yamanote line to Ikebukuro (east exit)

For Tokyoites who may not have the time or space to keep their own pets, Nekobukuro provides a venue for short-term cuddling with surrogate cats. Creep up to the 8th floor of the Ikebukuro branch of Tōkyū Hands (opposite) to get in on the kitten action.

>SHINJUKU

Shinjuku immediately immerses you into the sheer scale and manic energy of Tokyo, and thus makes the perfect introduction to the city. Shinjuku Station is Tokyo's largest hub, serving several major rail lines with an average of over 3.6 million commuters each day. Getting from A to B within the station can be akin to negotiating the levels of a chaotic videogame you've never played before – keep your eyes on the signs and you'll get where you need to go.

Above the station are the requisite gigantic department stores owned by major rail lines such as Odakyū and Keiō, and the Takashimaya Times Square complex to the south. Based in Nishi-Shinjuku (the west side) are the Tokyo Metropolitan Government Offices and a spate of luxury hotels catering to business folk, while Shinjuku's east side shows off a seedier angle in Tokyo's red-light district. The most well-known landmark on the east side is the Studio Alta building, an easy target for a meet-up in this lively quarter that many would consider downtown Tokyo.

SHINJUKU

◉ SEE
Hanazono-jinja 1 C3
Kabukichō 2 C2
Shinjuku-gyōen 3 D4
Tokyo Metropolitan
 Government Offices ...4 A4

🏠 SHOP
Beams 5 C3
Comme Ça 6 C3
Disk Union 7 C3
Don Quijote 8 C3
Isetan 9 C3
Journal Standard 10 C4
Kinokuniya 11 C4
Kinokuniya 12 C3
Marui Young 13 C3
Odakyū 14 B3

Sakuraya Camera 15 C3
Sekaido 16 D4
Tōkyū Hands 17 C4
Yodobashi Camera 18 B4

🍴 EAT
Chaya Macrobiotics .....(see 9)
Daidaiya 19 C3
Keika Kumamoto
 Rāmen 20 D3
Nakajima ....(see 5)
New York Grill 21 A4
Tokyo Dai Hanten 22 C3
Tsunahachi 23 C3

🅈 DRINK
Advocates Bar 24 D3
Arch ....(see 27)

Arty Farty 25 D3
Bar Plastic Model ......(see 26)
Bon's 26 C3
Kinswomyn 27 D3
La Jetée 28 C3
New York Bar ....(see 21)

⭐ PLAY
Green Plaza Ladies
 Sauna 29 C2
Loft 30 C2
National Nō Theatre
 (Kokuritsu
 Nō-Gakudō) 31 D6
Shinjuku Piccadilly 32 C3
Shinjuku Pit Inn 33 D3

◉ SEE

◉ HANAZONO-JINJA
花園神社

☎ 3200 3093; 5-17-3 Shinjuku, Shinjuku-ku; admission free; ⏰ dawn-dusk; ⓂMarunouchi & Toei Shinjuku lines to Shinjuku-sanchōme (exits B3 & B5)

Nestled in ultra-urban, high-rise Shinjuku is this quiet, unassuming shrine. Hanazono-jinja is particularly pleasant when it's lit up in the evening, but it also makes for a quick escape from the Kabukichō seediness. Sundays bring a flea market (open 8am to 4pm) to the shrine grounds, a good place to hunt for various vintage wares.

◉ KABUKICHŌ 歌舞伎町

Ⓙ JR Yamanote line to Shinjuku (east exit)

Kabukichō is Tokyo's red-light district, and it wears its gaudy neon bling on its sleeve. It's home to host clubs and soaplands ('massage' parlours) that the authorities are attempting to clean up, and *yakuza* (mafia) and wannabes do maintain a visible presence in the area. However, while Japanese people may warn you that it's a dangerous neighbourhood, never fear, taking the usual precautions after dark should suffice.

Beyond the golden sign, Tokyo's red-light district, Kabukichō, beckons with bright lights and bling

SPIRITED AWAY TO MITAKA

Visiting *anime* master Hayao Miyazaki's wondrous, imaginative **Ghibli Museum** (☎ 0422-40 2233; www.ghibli-museum.jp; 1-1-83 Shimo-Renjaku, Mitaka-shi; adult ¥1000, child ¥100-700; ☻ 10am-6pm Wed-Mon; ❹ JR Chūō line to Mitaka, south exit) is most easily arranged by reserving an appointment in advance (up to three months prior to your visit). If you can't plan that far ahead, it's possible – though slightly more complicated – to purchase tickets once you arrive in Tokyo (see the website for detailed ticketing information). The museum maintains a daily visitor quota and staggers admittance over two-hour blocks throughout the day – all for the sake of providing the most high-quality, least crowded experience for everyone.

A cute shuttle bus (one-way ¥200/100) runs from Mitaka Station to the museum if you'd prefer not to walk. But it's a flat 15-minute stroll from Mitaka, or a pleasant 20-minute walk from Inokashira Park (p92) in Kichijōji.

❻ SHINJUKU-GYŌEN
新宿御苑

☎ 3350 0151; 11 Naitochō, Shinjuku-ku; admission ¥200/50/free; ☻ 9am-4.30pm Tue-Sun; ❹ Marunouchi line to Shinjuku-gyōenmae (exit 1)

Dating back to 1906, this downtown park provides the perfect escape from winter cold, as it boasts a hothouse full of exotic tropical plants, allegedly even including peyote! There's also a French garden and a pond full of giant carp. Keep this park in mind when you're exhausted by all that busy Shinjuku has to offer.

❻ TOKYO METROPOLITAN GOVERNMENT OFFICES
東京都庁

☎ 5321 1111; 2-8-1 Nishi-Shinjuku, Shinjuku-ku; admission free; ☻ observatories 9.30am-11pm, north tower closed 2nd & 4th Mon, south tower closed 1st & 3rd Tue; ❹ Toei Ōedo line to Tochōmae (exits A3 & A4); ♿

Known as Tokyo Tochō, these colossal towers designed by Kenzō Tange comprise Tokyo's

AWESOME BLOSSOMS

Around April *sakura* (cherry blossom) fever grips the country with the pink-petalled flower emblazoning every surface that can be decorated: umbrellas, sake cups, hair accessories. The whole of Japan excitedly waits for the first buds to appear on cherry trees, and *hanami* (cherry-blossom viewing) parties pop up day and night to celebrate the flowers during their week-long flowering season. There's plenty of sake, singing and dancing at popular *hanami* spots, where the best sites are often taken by people who've camped out overnight for them. Good *hanami* spots include the Imperial Palace East Garden (p48) and Shinjuku-gyōen (left).

WORTH THE TRIP

On the western edge of Tokyo's 23 wards, **Kichijōji** is a short train ride from Shinjuku or Shibuya and makes an easy getaway for those suffering from urban overload. Kichijōji is one of Tokyo's most desirable neighbourhoods, with its university-town feel, understated hipness factor and high quality of living. Take a walk in the park, browse a few boutiques and finish off with a cocktail in one of the cool little local bars.

The centrepiece of Kichijōji is **Inokashira Park** (☎ 042-247 6900; Inokashira, Mitaka-shi; boat rentals ¥200; ☻ 24hr; 🚇 JR Chūō & Sōbu lines to Kichijōji, Park exit; 🚇 Keiō In-okashira line to Kichijōji, Park exit). The park is at its lively but low-key best on the weekends, when artists and musicians come out to play. Stroll the shaded edge of the small lake, visit the temple to Benzaiten (goddess of love and the arts), rent a paddle boat and feel the urban tension melt away. However, cherry-blossom season is the exception to the peaceful rule.

From Kichijōji Station, take the park exit and look for the Marui department store. Walk down the road to the right of the building, which will lead you down the gentle slope to the park. Take your time on the way down, and poke around the cafés, bohemian-style shops and ethnic restaurants lining the road.

If you have arranged an appointment at the Ghibli Museum (p91), an alternative way to get there is walking through the park from Kichijōji. Allow at least 20 minutes for the walk.

bureaucratic heartland. From the amphitheatrelike Citizen's Plaza below, check out the architecture and complex symmetry of the towers. Then whiz up to the twin observation decks, over 200m above urban Shinjuku, for a look at Tokyo below.

🏠 SHOP
🏠 BEAMS Fashion
☎ 5368 7300; www.beams.co.jp; 3-32-6 Shinjuku, Shinjuku-ku; ☻ 11am-8pm; 🚇 JR Yamanote line to Shinjuku (south exit)
The Beams chain has spread across Japan and over to Hong Kong, but all the best of Beams – from basic to superstylish men's and women's clothes, accessories, cool housewares and a gallery – has been concentrated into the seven floors of this Shinjukushop.

🏠 COMME ÇA Fashion
☎ 5367 5551; 3-26-6 Shinjuku, Shinjuku-ku; ☻ 11am-9pm Mon-Sat, 11am-8pm Sun; 🚇 JR Yamanote line to Shinjuku (east exit)
Provided you fit into local sizes, this branch of the Japanese chain has six floors of quality basics and inexpensive accessories. Plus: cake!

🔲 DISK UNION
ディスクユニオン *Music*

☎ 3352-2691; http://diskunion.net in Japanese; 3-31-4 Shinjuku, Shinjuku-ku; 🕙 11am-9pm Mon-Sat, 11am-8pm Sun; 🚉 JR Yamanote line (east exit)

This seven-storey branch has an excellent selection of CDs, both new and used. It has another branch on Shibuya (p122).

🔲 DON QUIJOTE
ドンキホーテ
Homewares & novelties

☎ 5291 9211; www.donki.com; 1-16-5 Kabukichō, Shinjuku-ku; 🕙 24hr; 🚉 JR Yamanote line to Shinjuku (east exit)

Meet Don Quijote, Tōkyū Hands' trashy cousin. In Kabukichō, the fluorescent-lit corner shop is filled to the brink with weird loot. Chaotic piles of knockoff electronics and designer goods sit alongside sex toys, fetish costumes and packaged foods. They have quite a presence in Tokyo, though not all shops are open 24 hours.

🔲 ISETAN 伊勢丹
Department store

☎ 3352 1111; 3-14-1 Shinjuku, Shinjuku-ku; 🕙 10am-8pm ⊕ Marunouchi & Toei Shinjuku lines to Shinjuku-sanchōme (exit A1)

In addition to having a stunning food basement, Isetan offers a free service called I-club, matching English-speaking staff to visiting shoppers; the membership desk is on the 6th floor of the main Isetan building. While you're there take a peek at the current exhibition in the 5th-floor art gallery.

🔲 JOURNAL STANDARD
Fashion

☎ 5367 0175; www.journal-standard .jp; 4-1-7 Shinjuku,Shinjuku-ku; 🕙 11.30am-8.30pm Mon-Fri, 11am-8pm Sat & Sun; 🚉 JR Yamanote line to Shinjuku (south exit)

Browsing the corners and surfaces of this hip shop turn up all sorts of items to add style to your wardrobe. Collections here are smart but bohemian, and sizes tend toward the Japanese figure (ie small). This is also a great place to end a shopping spree, as there's a lovely rooftop café on the 3rd floor.

🔲 KINOKUNIYA
紀伊國産書店 *Books*

☎ 5361 3301; Annexe Bldg, Takashimaya Times Square, 5-24-5 Sendagaya, Shibuya-ku; 🕙 10am-8pm Sun-Fri, 10am-8.30pm Sat; 🚉 JR Yamanote line to Shinjuku (new south exit)

Kinokuniya's large annexe store in the Takashimaya Times Square complex surpasses the main Shinjuku store (☎ 3354 0131; 3-17-7 Shinjuku, Shinjuku-ku; 🕙 10am-9pm; 🚉 JR Yamanote line to Shinjuku (east exit)), with its variety and depth of titles in English. Find foreign-language books on the 6th floor, and a rainy day's worth of art books, magazines and manga everywhere else.

🏬 MARUI YOUNG
マルイヤング
Department store
☎ 3354 0101; 3-18-1 Shinjuku, Shinjuku-ku; ⏰ 11.30am-9pm Mon-Sat, 11.30am-8.30pm Sun; 🚊 JR Yamanote line to Shinjuku (east exit)
You can't swing a coat hanger in Shinjuku without hitting a speciality branch of Marui (look for the Marui logo: OIOI). Marui Young is the place to begin shopping if you want to buy Goth-Lolita garb with the local whitest-shade-of-pale girls.

🏬 ODAKYŪ 小田急百貨店
Department store
☎ 3342 1111; 1-1-3 Nishi-Shinjuku, Shinjuku-ku; ⏰ shops 10am-8pm, restaurants 11am-10pm; 🚊 JR Yamanote line to Shinjuku (west exit)
The 16-floor behemoth of a department store that sits atop Shinjuku Station, Odakyū contains several restaurant floors, high-end boutiques and low-budget accessories shops, as well as just about anything you'd need to live inside the station for the next 10 years.

📷 SAKURAYA CAMERA
さくらやカメラ
Cameras & electronics
☎ 3352 4711; 3-2-6 Shinjuku, Shinjuku-ku; ⏰ 10am-10pm; 🚊 JR Yamanote line to Shinjuku (east exit)
One of the big three camera emporiums, Sakuraya Camera offers many of the same inventory as the others, at similar prices. It has an incredible selection of long lenses and tiny digital cameras. You'll find some great deals here but like anywhere, comparison shopping is essential.

🏬 SEKAIDO 世界堂
Stationery
☎ 5379 1111; 3-1-1 Shinjuku, Shinjuku-ku; ⏰ 9.30am-9pm; 🚇 Marunouchi & Toei Shinjuku lines to Shinjuku-sanchōme (exit C1)
Art-supply junkies should only visit Sekaido on a preset budget, as they're otherwise doomed to blow a fortune on the blindingly broad array of art supplies, exquisite *washi* (handmade paper) and vast selection of manga.

🏬 TŌKYŪ HANDS
東急ハンズ
Homewares & novelties
☎ 5361 3111; Takashimaya Times Square, 5-24-2 Sendagaya, Shibuya-ku; ⏰ 10am-8.30pm; 🚊 JR Yamanote line to Shinjuku (new south exit)
Ostensibly a do-it-yourself store, Tōkyū Hands carries a compre-

WORTH THE TRIP

Psst – wanna score some high-quality handicrafts? **Bingoya** (☎ 3202 8778; www.quasar.nu/bingoya; 10-6 Waka-matsuchō, Shinjuku-ku; ❧ 10am-7pm Tue-Sun; ◉ Toei Ōedo line to Waka-matsu-Kawada) may be just the ticket. It's only a couple of stops from Shinjuku to the sweet, unassuming neighbour-hood of Wakamatsuchō. Just a short stroll from the station (turn right from either exit), this friendly shop stocks regional ceramics, vibrant batik textiles, richly dyed washi (handmade paper), handmade glassware and tatami (woven floor mats) in five compact floors. They also accept credit cards.

hensive collection of everything you didn't know you needed, from blown-glass pens to chainsaws, tofu tongs to party supplies. The Takashimaya Times Square branch is probably the least maddening to shop in, but there are others in Shibuya (p124) and Ikebukuro (p86).

YODOBASHI CAMERA

ヨドバシカメラ

Cameras & electronics

☎ 3346 1010; 1-11-1 Nishi-Shinjuku, Shinjuku-ku; ❧ 9.30am-9.30pm; ◉ Toei Shinjuku line to Shinjuku (exit 5), ◉ JR Yamanote line to Shinjuku (west exit)

Yodobashi is Sakuraya's larg-est competitor and sits directly across the street. This store stocks anything from digital camcorders to secondhand enlargers. Prices at Yodobashi are very competitive, and if you can't dig it up here then it probably can't be found in Japan.

EAT

Although it's rumoured to be razed imminently, Omoide-yokochō (Memory Lane, or 'Piss Alley', as it's less politely known) might still be standing when you visit. Alongside the tracks just outside the west exit of Shinjuku station, this alley is lined with small stalls and rickety eateries. Round about evening rush hour, salarymen and labourers alike spill into these shops specialising variously in rāmen, yakitori or nabe to have a bite before braving their full-to-bursting trains home. It's a nostalgic taste of Occupation-era atmosphere – and it really isn't as pungent as its nickname might suggest.

CHAYA MACROBIOTICS

チャヤマクロビオティック

ス *Macrobiotic* ¥¥

☎ 3357 0014; 7F, Isetan Bldg, 3-14-1 Shinjuku, Shinjuku-ku; ❧ 11am-10pm; ◉ Marunouchi line to Shinjuku-sanchōme (exit A1); Ⓥ

Marrying the concepts of Japanese macrobiotics and French cuisine,

Chaya offers healthy whole foods alongside lists of organic tea, wine and French apple cider. Though the seasonal menu is anchored by mostly vegan offerings such as red rice risotto, seitan-and-millet burgers and seaweed side salads, fish also figures prominently. Desserts like the soy crème brûlée are a particular treat.

🍴 DAIDAIYA 橙家
Asian fusion   ¥¥

☎ 5362 7173; 3F, Shinjuku Nowa Bldg, 3-37-12 Shinjuku, Shinjuku-ku; 🕐 5pm-1am; 🚇 JR Yamanote line to Shinjuku (My City exit)

The happy fusion of neon with tatami in Daidaiya's décor parallels its deft commingling of both modern international cuisine with traditional Japanese dishes. The prix-fixe meals are a better deal than ordering à la carte, although if you're tempted to order wine (just give in), the point is moot.

🍴 KEIKA KUMAMOTO RĀMEN 桂花熊本ラーメン
Rāmen   ¥

☎ 3354 4591; 3-7-2 Shinjuku, Shinjuku-ku; 🕐 11am-11pm; 🚇 Marunouchi & Toei Shinjuku lines to Shinjuku-sanchōme (exit C4); ♿ 👶

The Kyūshū-style *tonkotsu rāmen* (pork broth–based noodles), is worth queuing for at this nationally famous *rāmen* shop. You

order and pay as you enter; try the *chāshū-men* (*rāmen* with sliced pork). There's no English sign, so look for the large, multicoloured cartoon mural of a chef and pigs on its exterior.

🍴 NAKAJIMA 中嶋
Traditional Japanese   ¥¥

☎ 3356 7962; http://shinjyuku-naka jima.com; 3-32-5 Shinjuku, Shinjuku-ku; 🕐 11.30am-2.30pm & 5.30-10pm Mon-Sat; 🚇 Marunouchi line to Shinjuku-sanchōme (exit A1)

Having garnered one Michelin star in 2008, Nakajima hasn't let this honour change its delicious ways. The house speciality is the *iwashi* (sardine) – whether simmered in sweet broth with egg, served as sashimi, or delicately fried and laid on a bed of rice, you can't go wrong. Down the alley next to the Beams building, look for a black building with an outside stairwell leading down to basement-level Nakajima.

🍴 NEW YORK GRILL ニューヨークグリル
American   ¥¥¥

☎ 5323 3458; 52F, Park Hyatt Tokyo, 3-7-1-2 Nishi-Shinjuku, Shinjuku-ku; 🕐 11.30am-midnight; 🚇 Toei Ōedo line to Tochōmae (exit A4); ♿ Ⓥ 👶

The drop-dead-delicious view notwithstanding, this sky-high spot continues to earn its reputation as one of Tokyo's top restaurants with its slabs of steak and racks of lamb. Worth waking for is the sumptuous daily brunch (¥6200; open 11.30am to 2.30pm), which on Sundays includes a glass of champagne. On the 1st floor, the New York Deli is lovely for a more casual lunch, with a delectable selection of fine cheeses, olives and cured meats.

▥ TOKYO DAI HANTEN
東京大飯店 *Yum cha*　　　　　¥

☎ 3202 0121 4F, Oriental Wave Bldg, 5-17-13 Shinjuku, Shinjuku-ku; ⏱ 11.30am-10pm; Ⓜ Marunouchi & Toei Shinjuku lines to Shinjuku-sanchōme (exits B3 & C6)

Established in 1960, Tokyo Dai Hanten is one of your few possibilities for *yum cha* (dim sum) and the place of choice for Hong Kong expats. Especially brisk and fresh are weekend brunches, served in the customary manner, with *yum cha* rolling by on trolleys for you to flag down at will.

▥ TSUNAHACHI つな八
Tempura　　　　　　　　　¥¥

☎ 3352 1012; 3-31-8 Shinjuku, Shinjuku-ku; ⏱ 11am-10pm; ◈ JR Yamanote line to Shinjuku (east exit); ♿ ♨

Sit at the counter for the pleasure of watching the efficient chefs fry each perfect tempura and plate them one by one. From Shinjuku-

dōri as you face Mitsukoshi department store, go down the small street to its left; Tsunahachi will be on your left. There is another, airier branch located on the 13th floor at Takashimaya Times Square.

▼ DRINK

You won't find another low-lying cluster of bars like the Golden Gai elsewhere in Tokyo; the atmosphere of each reveals something of its proprietor's personality, with some only small enough to accommodate a few patrons at a time. Note that some bars will only serve regular customers, but those we've listed welcome strangers.

Nearby, the Shinjuku-nichōme neighbourhood (known simply as Nichōme) has a thriving gay and lesbian scene, with gay bars filling out the nooks of these alleys. Keep your eyes peeled for signs in the windows; the bars around here are jammed in everywhere.

▼ ADVOCATES BAR
Gay & lesbian bar

☎ 3358 3988; 1F, Dai-7 Tenka Bldg, 2-18-1 Shinjuku, Shinjuku-ku; ⏱ 8pm-5am Mon-Sat, 8pm-1am Sun; Ⓜ Toei Shinjuku line to Shinjuku-sanchōme (exit C8)

Advocates Bar is just that – a bar, and a small one. As the crowd

Start your night at Advocates Bar (p97) and watch the crowds multiply and the drinks flow

gets bigger over the course of the evening, it overflows onto the street and becomes more like a block party. The staff here speaks English, and it's another good venue to start off a night in Nichōme.

☗ ARCH Gay & lesbian bar

☎ 3352 6297; www.clubarch.net; B1F, Dai-2 Hayakawaya Bldg, 2-14-6 Shinjuku, Shinjuku-ku; cover varies; ⏰ 8pm-4am; ⊖ Toei Shinjuku line to Shinjuku-sanchōme (exits C7 & C8)

At this fun club, you can relax with a mixed crowd, groove to what the DJ's spinning or cheer on the campy drag queens. Some nights are men- or women-only, so check the website before heading out.

☗ ARTY FARTY
アーティファーティ
Gay & lesbian bar

☎ 5362 9720; www.arty-farty.net; 2F, 2-11-7 Shinjuku, Shinjuku-ku; ⏰ 7pm-late Mon-Sat, 5pm-3am Sun; ⊖ Toei Shinjuku line to Shinjuku-sanchōme (exits C5 & C8)

Arty Farty is another stalwart of the queer scene, and has good all-you-can-drink specials. There's a reason it has been around for so long and it's a tried-and-true (although often incredibly crowded) place to start your evening and get the lowdown on what else is happening in the neighbourhood.

☒ BAR PLASTIC MODEL
バープラスチックモデル
Bar

☎ 5273 8441; www.plastic-model.net in Japanese; 1-1-10 Kabukichō, Shinjuku-ku; cover ¥700; ⏰ 8pm-5am Mon-Sat, 8pm-2am Sun; ⊕ Marunouchi line to Shinjuku-sanchōme (exit B5)

This is one of the new incarnations of Golden Gai bars, run by the next generation of bar owners and decorated with *tchotchkes* (knick-knacks) c 1980. There's sometimes a DJ here spinning beats.

☒ BON'S ボンズ *Bar*

☎ 3209 6334; 1-1-10 Kabukichō, Shinjuku-ku; cover ¥900; ⏰ 7pm-5am; ⊕ Marunouchi line to Shinjuku-sanchōme (exit B5)

Drinks start at ¥700 at this sure-fire spot in the Golden Gai. Look for its corner location with 'Old Fashioned American Style Pub' painted across its exterior wall.

☒ KINSWOMYN
キンズウミン
Gay & lesbian bar

☎ 3354 8720; 3F, Daiichi Tenka Bldg, 2-15-10 Shinjuku, Shinjuku-ku; cocktails ¥750; ⏰ 8pm-4am Wed-Mon; ⊕ Toei Shinjuku line to Shinjuku-sanchōme (exit C8)

Counterbalancing some of the more male-dominated gay bars in the neighbourhood, Kinswo-

myn is a popular and welcoming lesbian bar run by well-known activist Tara. It's perfect for visitors as English is spoken, and it's a comfortable environment for Japanese and foreign women alike.

☒ LA JETÉE ラジェッテイ
Bar

☎ 3208 9645; 1-1-8 Kabukichō, Shinjuku-ku; cover ¥700; ⏰ 7pm till late Mon-Sat; ⊕ Marunouchi line to Shinjuku-sanchōme (exit B5)

A favourite in the Golden Gai, Le Jetée is run by a French-speaking cinema buff and was given the name of a classic film. It's a good introduction to the singular culture of these alleys.

☒ NEW YORK BAR
ニューヨークバー *Bar*

☎ 5323 3458; www.parkhyatttokyo .com; 3-7-1-2 Nishi-Shinjuku, Shinjuku-ku; cover after 8pm ¥2000; ⏰ 5pm-midnight Sun-Wed, 5pm-1am Thu-Sat; ⊕ Toei Ōedo line to Tochōmae (exit A4)

Located in the stratosphere, both physically and socially, the New York Bar towers over the city on the 52nd floor of the Park Hyatt Tokyo in west Shinjuku. With magnificent views, strong drinks and live jazz, this is a swank lounge for that special date.

PLAY

⭐ GREEN PLAZA LADIES SAUNA グリーンプラザレディズサウナ *Public bath*

☎ 3207 5411; 9F, 1-29-2 Kabuki-chō, Shinjuku-ku; admission 6am-10pm ¥2700, 10pm-6am ¥3300; ⏰ 24hr; 🚉 JR Yamanote line to Shinjuku (east exit)

Women also have a place to wash and crash in Kabukichō. This central, 24-hour *sentō* (public bath) and spa for women is a calming refuge, where you can get a massage after you bathe, have a tasty bite to eat, and then blissfully snooze away until the morning trains begin running. Best of all, there's also a rooftop *rotemburo* (outdoor bath).

⭐ LOFT ロフト *Live music*

☎ 5272 0382; www.loft-prj.co.jp/LOFT/index.html; B2F, Tatehana Bldg, 1-12-9 Kabukichō, Shinjuku-ku; from ¥1000; ⏰ 5pm-late; 🚉 JR Yamanote line to Shinjuku (east exit)

This loud and smoky Shinjuku institution is a blast on a good night. Although it's a typically small venue, it draws both local and international acts ranging from punk to emo.

⭐ NATIONAL NŌ THEATRE 国立能楽堂 *Theatre*

☎ 3423 1331; 4-18-1 Sendagaya, Shibuya-ku; tickets ¥2800-5600; ⏰ reservations 10am-6pm; 🚉 Chūō & Sōbu lines to Sendagaya (west exit)

The National Nō Theatre stages its own *nō* (classical Japanese musical dramas) performances on weekends only, for which it provides printed English synopses, but it also hosts privately sponsored performances. Exit Sendagaya Station in the direction of Shinjuku on the left and follow the road that hugs the railway tracks; the theatre will be on the left.

MANGA KISSA

Kissaten (coffee shops) have long been mainstays for socialising away from home, but the next-generation versions are serious escape hatches. *Manga kissa* (comic-book cafés) are a great place to get inexpensive internet access in a comfy private cubicle. You can also browse their manga library, get a bite to eat, watch DVDs or catch some Zs. *Manga kissa* are open 24 hours per day, and you can prepay for as little as 30 minutes or, if you get caught out after midnight when the trains stop running, overnight. Rates are typically around ¥2500 for eight hours. See p198 for listings.

SENTŌ PRIMER

First you'll pay the *sentō* (public bath) fee to an attendant at the front desk, then head into the men's or women's changing room. In the changing room, place your clothes in one of the lockers and your toiletries in a *senmenki* (wash basin) and head into the bath area.

Before stepping into the bath, you'll need to wash at the banks of low showers and water spigots that line the walls. Grab a low stool and scrub thoroughly, making sure you remove all traces of soap so as not to cloud the water. Circulate between the hot tubs, cold pool, sauna and electric bath (which supposedly simulates the sensation of swimming with electric eels). If you soak everything just right, you'll float out in the desired state of *yudedako* ('boiled octopus').

★ SHINJUKU PICCADILLY 新宿ピカデリー *Cinema*

☎ 5367-1144; www.shinjukupiccadilly .com in Japanese; 3-15-15 Shinjuku, Shinjuku-ku; tickets from ¥1300/800; Ⓜ Marunouchi & Toei Shinjuku lines to Shinjuku-sanchōme (exits B7 & B8); ♿

Making its debut in July 2008, Tokyo's latest, greatest cinema experience features a gleaming, translucent white exterior and interior. The theatre itself boasts over 600 seats, including several two-person private viewing booths outfitted with surround sound and leather sofas (¥30,000 per screening, or ¥3,000,000 per year for high rollers).

★ SHINJUKU PIT INN 新宿ピットイン *Live music*

☎ 3354 2024; www.pit-inn.com/index _e.html; B1F, Accord Bldg, 2-12-14 Shinjuku, Shinjuku-ku; cover ¥1300-4000; ⏱ performances 2.30pm & 8pm; Ⓜ Toei Shinjuku line to Shinjuku-sanchōme (exits C5 & C6)

Shinjuku Pit Inn is one of the more well-established jazz clubs in Tokyo, showcasing the talents of both foreign and local jazz musicians. The jazz could be generally categorised as classically mainstream. Phone ahead for reservations. The cover includes one drink.

>HARAJUKU & AOYAMA

Travelling from Harajuku to Aoyama takes you from pop culture consumption to upscale, grown-up refinement. From the Harajuku JR station, take the Takeshita exit to Takeshita-dōri, a treasure-trove of teenybopper accessories and hair salons that can kink strait-laced hair into dreads and 'fros. Or exit to Omote-sandō, the boulevard lined with branches of Chanel, Prada and Tokyo's favourite: Louis Vuitton. You'll also come across the slanted walkways of the neighbourhood's newest shopping centre, Omotesandō Hills.

On either side of Omote-sandō, Ura-Hara (a nickname for the back alleys of Harajuku) hides tiny European-style cafés, innovative art galleries, restaurants and boutiques catering both to youth and moneyed sophisticates. The further southeast you travel down Omote-sandō, the closer you'll get to Aoyama, where internationally recognised home-grown designers have based their flagships. And if your credit card has rolled over and is playing dead, you can at least window-shop and watch the live fashion walking the streets.

HARAJUKU & AOYAMA

Please see over for map

SEE

LAFORET MUSEUM HARAJUKU ラフォーレミュージアム原宿

☎ 6406 6378; www.lapnet.jp/index.html in Japanese; 6F, Laforet Bldg, 1-11-6 Jingūmae, Shibuya-ku; admission varies; ⏰ 11am-8pm; 🚃 JR Yamanote line to Harajuku (Omote-sandō exit), 🚇 Chiyoda line to Meiji-jingūmae (exit 5); ♿

This museum, on the 6th floor of the teenybopper fashionista mecca that is Laforet department store, is gallery or performance space depending on the event. Small film festivals, art installations and launch parties are held here regularly – after browsing the art-as-streetwear on the floors below, check out art-as-art upstairs.

MEIJI-JINGŪ 明治神宮

☎ 3379 5511; www.meijijingu.or.jp; 1-1 Yoyogi Kamizonochō, Shibuya-ku; admission free; ⏰ dawn-dusk; 🚃 JR Yamanote line to Harajuku (Omote-sandō exit)

In the grounds of Meiji-jingū, **Meiji-jingū-gyoen** (admission ¥500/200; ⏰ 9am-4.30pm), is a beautiful garden created by Emperor Meiji as a gift to the Empress Shōken. There's also a **Treasure Museum** (admission ¥300; ⏰ 9am-4pm Sat, Sun & public holidays) on the grounds, displaying some imperial artefacts such as ceremonial clothing worn by the emperor and empress.

NEZU MUSEUM

☎ 3400 2536; www.nezu-muse.or.jp; 6-5-1 Minami-Aoyama, Minato-ku; admission ¥1000/700; ⏰ 9.30am-4pm Tue-Sun; 🚇 Chiyoda, Ginza, Hanzōmon lines to Omote-sandō (exits A4 & A5)

By publication time, the Nezu collection of Asian art should be open for viewing in a completely rebuilt museum. If, against the odds, the lovely Japanese garden has been left untouched, the outdoor space provides an airy complement to the works inside.

ŌTA MEMORIAL ART MUSEUM 太田記念美術館

☎ 3403 0880; www.ukiyoe-ota-muse.jp/english.html; 1-10-10 Jingūmae, Shibuya-ku; admission ¥1000/700; ⏰ 10.30am-5.30pm Tue-Sun, closed from 27th to end of each month; 🚃 JR Yamanote line to Harajuku (Omote-sandō exit), 🚇 Chiyoda line to Meiji-jingūmae (exit 5)

Leave your shoes in the foyer and pad in slippers through this museum to view its stellar collection of ukiyo-e (wood-block prints), which includes works by masters including Hiroshige and Hokusai. There's an extra charge for special exhibits. The museum is up the hill on a narrow road behind Laforet; there's a clear map on the museum's website.

PRADA AOYAMA
プラダ青山

☎ 6418 0400; 5-2-6 Minami-Aoyama, Minato-ku; ⏰ 11am-8pm; ⊕ Chiyoda, Ginza & Hanzōmon lines to Omote-sandō (exits A4 & A5)
Of course you could shop here, but you can also ogle the gorgeous, convex glass bubbles of the exterior. Designed by Herzog & de Meuron, this is one of Aoyama's sexier organic-looking structures.

SPIRAL BUILDING
スパイラルビル

☎ 3498 1171; 5-6-23 Minami-Aoyama, Minato-ku; admission free; ⏰ 11am-8pm; ⊕ Chiyoda, Ginza & Hanzōmon lines to Omote-sandō (exit B1); ♿

Its asymmetrical, geometric shape may not look very sinuous on the outside, but the Spiral Building's name will make more sense upon entry. The 1st-floor gallery features changing exhibits, shows, dining and a CD-listening station. Check out the shop on the 2nd floor for art books, jewellery, *washi* (handmade paper) and stylishly designed loot.

TŌGŌ-JINJA 東郷神社

☎ 3403 3591; 1-5-3 Jingūmae, Shibuya-ku; admission free; ⏰ 6am-8pm; ⊕ JR Yamanote line to Harajuku (Takeshita exit)
This small shrine was built as a memorial to Admiral Tōgō Heihachiro, who led a pivotal battle against the

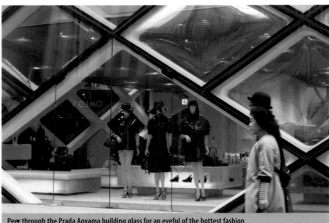
Peer through the Prada Aoyama building glass for an eyeful of the hottest fashion

DESIGN FESTA

Nowadays the biannual Design Festa happens in May and December at the Tokyo International Exhibition Centre, more fondly known as Tokyo Big Sight (p157). Hundreds of young, undiscovered artists and designers, including budding fashion designers, performance artists, filmmakers and musicians, rent spaces in the massive West Hall to reveal the fruits of their creative genius. Design Festa is *the* place to get a good idea of what Tokyo's working artists are doing, and to get your paws on a one-off T-shirt or piece of jewellery. If you're not in town for Design Festa, check out the insanely embellished **Design Festa Gallery** (☎ 3479 1442; www.designfestagallery.com; 3-20-18 Jingūmae, Shibuya-ku; admission free; ⏰ 11am-8pm), which is open year-round except during Design Festa.

Russians in 1905. These days, the shrine grounds are the venue for a flea market on the 1st, 4th and 5th Sunday of each month. Wares on sale include vintage kimonos, antiques and curios. The market usually winds down around 3pm.

◉ WATARI MUSEUM OF CONTEMPORARY ART
ワタリウム美術館
☎ 3402 3001; www.watarium.co.jp in Japanese; 3-7-6 Jingūmae, Shibuya-ku; ¥1000/800; ⏰ 11am-7pm Tue-Sun
🚇 Ginza line to Gaienmae (exit 3)
Known as the Watarium, this place showcases lots of brilliant conceptual and performance art, with visiting Scandinavians choreographing ballets involving vacuum-cleaners, and resident Japanese embalming themselves with glue. Ergo, lots of cutting-edge contemporary art can be found here, especially mixed-media art installations.

◉ YOYOGI-KŌEN
代々木公園
☎ 3469 6081; 2-1 Yoyogi Kamizonochō, Shibuya-ku; admission free;
⏰ 24hr; 🚇 JR Yamanote line to Harajuku (Omote-sandō exit); 🚇 Chiyoda line to Yoyogi-kōen (exit 4); ♿
The 54 hectares of Yoyogi Park (p23) were originally developed as part of the 1964 Olympic Village and was established as a city park in 1967. From the Harajuku JR

FREE CYCLING
You don't have to brave Tokyo road traffic (nor even bring your own bicycle) to take a leisurely ride on some fair-weather weekend. On Sundays 500 rental bicycles are available free on a first-come, first-served basis both at the **Imperial Palace East Garden** (p48; ⏰ 9am-3pm) and the approximately 2.5km path at **Jingū-gaien** (Map p105; ⏰ 9am-4pm), when the roads are closed to motorised vehicles.

station, exit right and turn right again, then follow the road along the edge of park until you reach an entry on your right. Across the road, look for the dramatic swooping lines of the National Yoyogi Gymnasium.

SHOP

🛍 BAPEXCLUSIVE
ベイプエクスクルーシヴ
Fashion
☎ 3407 2145; 5-5-8 Minami-Aoyama, Minato-ku; ⏰ 11am-7pm; 🚇 Chiyoda, Ginza, Hanzōmon lines to Omote-sandō (exit A5)
BAPE (A Bathing Ape) is no longer the madly exclusive brand that made it so desirable – this shop is testament to how underground designer Nigo's brand *isn't*, but how wildly successful it's become. BAPE has a dozen or so 'secret', hard-to-find shops around Harajuku and Aoyama; this one's a good starting point for brand fans and architecture buffs.

🛍 COMME DES GARÇONS
コムデギャルソン *Fashion*
☎ 3406 3951; 5-2-1 Minami-Aoyama, Minato-ku; ⏰ 11am-8pm; 🚇 Chiyoda, Ginza & Hanzōmon lines to Omote-sandō (exit A4)
When Rei Kawakubo hit interna-tional recognition status in the early

'80s, it was with her revolutionary, minimalist, matte black designs. Her lines have evolved from that simple chic, but even with asymmetrical cuts, illusions of torn fabric and sleeves gone missing, her style is consistently a departure from the norm. This Aoyama architectural wonder is her flagship store.

🛍 CONDOMANIA
コンドマニア
Homewares & novelties
☎ 3797 6131; 6-30-1 Jingūmae, Shibuya-ku; ⏰ 10.30am-11pm; 🚆 JR Yamanote line to Harajuku (Omote-sandō exit), 🚇 Chiyoda line to Meiji-jingūmae (exit 4)
Inside this tiny shop you'll find more condoms than you can poke a… stick at. For your love-hotel ex-peditions or footloose friends back home, pick up enigmatic prophy-lactics such as the 'Masturbator's Condom' or the more conservative glow-in-the-dark variety.

🛍 DAISO ダイソー
Homewares & novelties
☎ 5775 9641; Village 107 Bldg, 1-19-24 Jingūmae, Shibuya-ku; ⏰ 10am-9pm; 🚆 JR Yamanote line to Harajuku (Takeshita exit)
When Japan's economy crashed, *hyakkin* (100-yen shops) began raking in the cash…and haven't stopped. Among the hundreds in

Catch the hipsters and cutting-edge fashion of Laforet (p111)

Tokyo, Daiso is easily accessible and stocked with four floors full of merchandise costing ¥100. It's a great souvenir stop, where you can find rice bowls painted with cute animals, vampiric nail polish and random, silly kitsch.

☐ FUJI-TORII 富士鳥居
Art & antiques

☎ 3400 2777; www.fuji-torii.com; 6-1-10 Jingūmae, Shibuya-ku; ⏰ 11am-6pm Wed-Mon, closed every 3rd Mon; ⊕ Chiyoda line to Meiji-jingūmae (exit 4)

This reliable antique dealer has been in the business since 1948

and stocks everything from exquisite *kutani* (regional ceramics featuring striking enamel designs) to inexpensive modern wood-block prints. It has an especially good selection of beautiful *byōbu* (antique folding screens).

☐ HANAE MORI BUILDING
ハナエモリビル
Art & antiques

B1F, 3-6-1 Kita-Aoyama, Minato-ku; ⏰ 11am-7pm; ⊕ Chiyoda, Ginza, Hanzōmon lines to Omote-sandō (exit A1)

In Harajuku, the basement of the Hanae Mori building has more ...

than 30 antique shops hawking everything from over-the-hill kewpie dolls to cloisonné bracelets and antique obi ornaments.

📷 HYSTERIC GLAMOUR ヒステリックグラモー
Fashion

☎ 3409 7227; www.hystericglamour.jp in Japanese; 6-23-2 Jingūmae, Shibuya-ku; ⏰ 11am-8pm; 🚇 JR Yamanote line to Harajuku (Omote-sandō exit), 🚇 Chiyoda line to Meiji-jingūmae (exit 4)

It's more attitudinal tongue-in-cheek than hysterical or glamorous, but whatever you want to call it, it's fun stuff spiked generously with that Tokyo flavour. There's even a toddler line, the ultimate in designer punk for your little rocker. Design junkies will want to check out the curvy, futuristic branch at Roppongi Hills.

📷 ISSEY MIYAKE 三宅一生
Fashion

☎ 3423 1407; 3-18-11 Minami-Aoyama, Minato-ku; ⏰ 10am-8pm; 🚇 Chiyoda, Ginza & Hanzōmon lines to Omote-sandō (exit 4)

Anarchic but wearable conceptual fashion continues to flow from Issey Miyake. At the cluster of Aoyama shops along the south end of Omote-sandō, eye his famous pleated designs, or the

A-POC garments – each made from a single piece of fabric. The gallerylike window displays are worth a look, after checking out the many-faceted Prada spaceship down the street.

📷 KASŪKŌBŌ かすう工房
Jewellery & accessories

☎ 3479 3150; 4-28-14 Meiji-jingūmae, Shibuya-ku; ⏰ noon-8pm; 🚇 JR Yamanote line to Harajuku (Takeshita exit); 🚇 Chiyoda line to Meiji-jingūmae (exit 5)

This open-air jewellery shop on a raised platform has an old-fashioned feel even while the tattooed dude kneeling behind the display cases exudes the casual air of the modern Ura-Hara denizen. Mostly sculpted silver jewellery with themes of lotuses, dragons and *koi* (carp), the pieces here are simultaneously fresh and modern.

📷 KIDDYLAND キディランド *Toys*

☎ 3409 3431; www.kiddyland.co.jp; 6-1-9 Jingūmae, Shibuya-ku; ⏰ 10am-8pm, closed 3rd Tue of each month; 🚇 Chiyoda line to Meiji-jingūmae (exit 4)

Eep! Six floors of *kawaii* (cute) paraphernalia for your children – or, let's face it, you – to fall in lust with. Stuffed with stuffed animals, a candy-store selection of hair baubles, 200-yen toy vending machines, an abundance of Hello Kitty products, plastic action figures and noisy games, this store can be dangerously tempting (and *very* crowded on weekends).

🏠 LAFORET ラフォーレ
Fashion

☎ 3475 0411; 1-11-6 Jingūmae, Shibuya-ku; 🕐 11am-8pm; 🚃 JR Yamanote line to Harajuku (Omote-sandō exit)

Expressing identity and individuality is a function of fashion, and Tokyo youth are famous for taking this concept to the next level. Sample this in action at Laforet; surveying the shoppers is equal to the window-shopping, and once you've got the hang of the half-floor concept, you can count your way up to the 6th-floor museum (p103).

🏠 ON SUNDAYS *Books*

☎ 3470 1424; www.watarium.co.jp in Japanese; 3-7-6 Jingūmae, Shibuya-ku; 🕐 11am-8pm Tue-Sun; 🚇 Ginza line to Gaienmae (exit 3)

Connected to Watari Museum of Contemporary Art (p107), On Sundays carries an eclectic collection of avant-garde art for sale. It has a humongous selection of funky to classic postcards, and a marvellous

array of functional arthouse objects, such as purses in the shapes of origami balloons and Scandinavian-style office accoutrements. In the basement is a wonderful café/bookshop.

🏠 ORIENTAL BAZAAR
オリエンタルバザー
Handicrafts

☎ 3400 3933; 5-9-13 Jingūmae, Shibuya-ku; 🕐 10am-7pm Fri-Wed; 🚇 Chiyoda line to Meiji-jingūmae (exit 4)

Carrying a wide-ranging selection of antiques and souvenirs at very reasonable prices, Oriental Bazaar is a great spot for last-minute, one-stop gift shopping. Among the wares are fans, folding screens, pottery, porcelain and *yukata* (cotton kimono). The branch at Narita Airport opens at 7.30am if you need to offload some yen predeparture.

🏠 SOU-SOU そうそう
Fashion

☎ 3407 7877; 2F, from 1st Bldg, 5-3-10 Minami-Aoyama, Minato-ku; 🕐 11am-8pm; 🚇 Chiyoda, Ginza, Hanzōmon lines to Omote-sandō (exit A5)

Details matter to Japanese fashionistas – socks included. Contemporary *tabi* (split-toe socks) are sold all over Tokyo in endless patterns and colours.

Sou-Sou designs its high-quality *tabi* with playful style, in addition to producing serious footwear like steel-toed, rubber-soled *tabi* worn by Japanese construction workers.

🏠 TSUKIKAGEYA 月影屋 *Fashion*

☎ 3465 7111; www.tsukikageya .com; 1-9-19 Tomigaya, Shibuya-ku; 🕐 noon-8pm Thu-Mon; 🚇 Chiyoda line to Yoyogi-kōen (exit 2)

So you want to go to a *matsuri* (temple festival) all dolled up in a traditional *yukata* (cotton kimono), but you're more punk rock than Hello Kitty? Then head to Tsukikageya for black-and-white *yukata,* along with Swarovski-studded or snakeskin accessories. See also p114.

🏠 TSUMORI CHISATO ツモリチサト *Fashion*

☎ 3423 5170; 4-21-25 Minami-Aoyama, Minato-ku; 🕐 11am-8pm; 🚇 Chiyoda, Ginza & Hanzōmon lines to Omote-sandō (exit A4)

After working under Issey Miyake, designer Tsumori Chisato launched her own line in 1990 with the blessing of her mentor. Now she designs fun and well-tailored clothing that falls gracefully along the lines of the body, while retaining a whimsical aesthetic, using beading, embroidery and eye-catching appliqué.

🏠 UNDERCOVER *Fashion*

☎ 3407 1232; 5-3-18 Minami-Aoyama, Minato-ku; 🕐 11am-8pm; 🚇 Chiyoda, Ginza & Hanzōmon lines to Omote-sandō (exit A5)

Former punk-band frontman Jun Takahashi's take on youth-minded streetwear is still pretty crazy after all this time. His Undercover Lab, designed by architect Astrid Klein, is just up and across the street from Tsumori Chisato.

🏠 YOHJI YAMAMOTO 耀司山本 *Fashion*

☎ 3409 6006; 5-3-6 Minami-Aoyama, Minato-ku; 🕐 11am-8pm; 🚇 Chiyoda, Ginza & Hanzōmon lines to Omote-sandō (exit A4)

Yohji Yamamoto has maintained some mystery of himself and his aesthetic, flouting convention decade after decade in a mischievous way that keeps his style fresh – a feat when your colour of choice is black. He is one of the locals who has set up house here in Aoyama.

🍽 EAT

🍽 FONDA DE LA MADRUGADA フォンダデラマドゥルガーダ *Mexican* ¥¥¥

☎ 5410 6288; B1F, Villa Blanca, 2-33-11 Jingūmae, Shibuya-ku; 🕐 5.30pm-2am Sun-Thu, 5.30pm-5am Fri & Sat; 🚃 JR Yamanote line to Harajuku (Takeshita exit); 🍴

Fonda de la Madrugada makes the best Mexican food in Tokyo and is a favourite with expats. Complete with open courtyards and mariachi musicians, everything from the roof tiles to the chefs has been imported from Mexico. It's not cheap, but the enchiladas are worth it.

🍴 FUJIMAMAS フジママス
Asian fusion ¥¥
☎ 5485 2283; www.fujimamas.com; 6-3-2 Jingūmae, Shibuya-ku; ⏲ 11am-11pm; ⊖ Chiyoda line to Meiji-Jingūmae (exit 4), 🚃 JR Yamanote line to Harajuku (Omote-sandō exit); 👤 Ⓥ 👤

Fujimamas is hugely popular for its Asian-fusion cuisine – such as par-seared salmon with wasabi cream – and its quality Californian wines. Upstairs are airy rooms in what was once a tatamimaker's workshop. Fujimamas also offers a great children's menu. The restaurant is in the first alley south of the Omote-sandō and Meiji-jingū intersection. Reservations are recommended.

🍴 HIROBA 広場
Organic vegetarian ¥
☎ 3406 6409; B1F, Crayon House Bldg, 3-8-15 Kita-Aoyama, Minato-ku; ⏲ 11am-10pm; ⊖ Chiyoda, Ginza & Hanzōmon lines to Omote-sandō (exits B2 & B4); 👤 Ⓥ 👤

Hiroba is a veritable vegetarian oasis, particularly if you go for the lunch buffet (¥1260). The organic Japanese buffet includes both vegetarian and meat options; descriptions are only in Japanese but signs for each dish include cute, helpful drawings of fish or pigs to explain if animal ingredients were used. The building is off Omote-sandō, a block behind the Hanae Mori building.

🍴 KINOKUNIYA 紀ノ国屋
International groceries
☎ 3409 1231; www.super-kinokuniya .jp; B1F, AO Bldg, 3-11-7 Kita-Aoyama, Minato-ku; ⏲ 9.30am-9pm; ⊖ Chiyoda, Ginza, Hanzōmon lines to Omote-sandō (exit B2)

Kinokuniya carries expat lifesavers such as Marmite and peanut butter, Belgian chocolate and herbal tea. Foreign imports including cheese, salami and Finnish bread generally fetch high prices, much like the flawless fruit in the produce section. It's moved back to its original location, now in the basement of the glitzy new AO Building.

🍴 LAS CHICAS ラスチカス
Cafe ¥
☎ 3407 6865; 5-47-6 Jingūmae, Shibuya-ku; ⏲ 11.30am-11pm Mon-Thu, 11am-11.30pm Fri & Sat, 11am-11pm Sun; ⊖ Chiyoda, Ginza & Hanzōmon lines to Omote-sandō (exit B2); 👤 Ⓥ 👤

Natsuki Shigeta
Designer of rock-and-roll yukata (cotton kimono) at Tsukikageya (p112)

What inspires your designs? I create what I'd want to wear myself, but I want those same designs – lips, hearts, stars – to be worn by men. The hot-pink accessories started with the nail colour I've worn for several years. I also created a series of obi (kimono sashes) printed from my own photographs. My photo of the lights of Ginza at night came out pink – not my intention, but it matched perfectly! **Who are your clientele?** About half are super-fashionable 20-somethings; the other half are kimono freaks from their 40s upward. Ninety-five percent are men. The young generation is fashion-crazy; many have never worn *yukata* and consider wearing them sort of radical. **Where is your favourite part of Tokyo to shop for clothes?** I *never* go shopping! But when I'm selling at Laforet (p111) during the summer, it's interesting to see what's going on there.

Chill out on one of the coolest terraces in Tokyo – at Las Chicas, popular with expats and a hip, arty Aoyama crowd. Along with espresso drinks and fine wines, the menu is composed of casual classics such as the Caligula salad (Caesar with a twist). Having reopened in 2008, the new Las Chicas complex has lost none of its appeal in the revamp.

⊞ LE BRETAGNE
ルブルターニュ French ¥¥
☎ 3478 7855; 3-5-4 Jingūmae, Shibuya-ku; ⏲ 11.30am-11pm Mon-Sat, 11.30am-10pm Sun; ⊕ Chiyoda, Ginza & Hanzōmon lines to Omote-sandō (exit A2); ⚅ V ♿
Le Bretagne's wonderful set menus, with their buckwheat *galettes* as the centrepieces, are authentic and filling. The sweet or savoury Breton-style crêpes can also be ordered à la carte for mere pocket change – money well-spent on these fresh and tasty creations.

⊞ MAISEN まい泉
Japanese ¥
☎ 3470-0071; 4-8-5 Jingūmae, Shibuya-ku; ⏲ 11am-10pm; ⊕ Chiyoda, Ginza, Hanzōmon lines to Omote-sandō (exit A2)
Maisen is famous for its crispy and tender *tonkatsu* (deep-fried pork cutlets) that draws a continuous crowd. Thankfully, the place occupies a converted bathhouse,

so there's plenty of room for the many hungry souls craving Kagoshima *kurobuta* (black pig). If you're on the run, pick up a *bentō* (boxed meal) at the takeaway window.

⊞ MOMINOKI HOUSE
モミノキハウス
Organic vegetarian ¥¥
☎ 3405 9144; www2.odn.ne.jp /mominoki_house; 1F, YOU Bldg, 2-18-5 Jingūmae, Shibuya-ku; ⏲ noon-10.30pm; ⊕ JR Yamanote line to Harajuku, Takeshita exit); V
For herbivorous relief, stop into Mominoki House, where the largely macrobiotic menu covers the vegan to the vegetarian. There's also free-range organic chicken for the carnivorously inclined. The rambling space is cosily welcoming, as is the friendly chef-owner.

⊞ NATARAJ ナタラジ
Indian ¥¥
☎ 5474 0510; www.nataraj.co.jp; B1F, 2-22-19 Minami-Aoyama, Minato-ku; ⏲ 11.30am-3pm & 5.30-11pm Mon-Fri, 11.30am-11pm Sat & Sun; ⊕ Ginza line to Gaienmae (exit B1); V
Nataraj's Aoyama restaurant has a warm and slightly more upscale atmosphere than many Indian joints in the city, but more notable is its excellent vegetarian cuisine.

NEIGHBOURHOODS

HARAJUKU & AOYAMA

🍴 NATURAL HARMONY ANGOLO ナチュラルハーモニーアンゴロ
Organic vegetarian ¥¥

☎ 3405 8393; 1F, Puzzle Aoyama Bldg, 3-38-12 Jingūmae, Shibuya-ku; ⏰ 11.30am-2.30pm & 5.30-9.30pm ⓜ Ginza line to Gaienmae (exit 2); Ⓥ ♿

Refreshingly smoke-free and dishing up live foods and excellent vegetarian fare, Natural Harmony is Tokyo's best-known natural-food spot. Tall salads, creamy risottos and organic beer and sake entice those who trek to this veggie haven; the menu is largely vegetarian, but fish and meat dishes augment the menu.

🍴 UME-NO-HANA 梅の花
Traditional Japanese ¥¥¥

☎ 3475 8077; 6F, Aoyama Bell Commons, 2-14-6 Kita-aoyama, Minato-ku; ⏰ 11am-3pm & 5-9pm Mon-Sat, 5-10pm Sun; ⓜ Ginza & Hanzōmon lines (exit 2)

This traditional, elegant restaurant is rightfully well-known for its *kai-seki* (elegant, multicourse Japanese meals) meals that showcase tofu and *yuba* (tofu 'skin') in beautifully presented small courses. Both *niku-nashi* (vegetarian) and meat-inclusive sets are available, but ordering will be problematic unless you have a Japanese speaker make the reservation for you and help you decide the best set for you and your party.

🍸 DRINK
🍸 DEN AQUAROOM デンアクアルーム *Lounge*

☎ 5778 2090; B1F, 5-13-3 Minami-Aoyama, Minato-ku; cover ¥700; ⏰ 6pm-2am Mon-Sat, 6-11pm Sun; ⓜ Chiyoda, Ginza, Hanzōmon lines to Omote-sandō (exit B1)

Darting fish within the walls of backlit, blue aquariums make a visual counterpoint to the bop of jazz bass-lines. Even prettier than the dark décor is the chic clientele floating around in here.

🍸 TOKYO APARTMENT CAFÉ 東京アパートメントカフェ *Lounge*

☎ 3401 4101; 1-11-11 Jingūmae, Shibuya-ku; ⏰ 11am-4am; ⓜ Chiyoda line to Meiji-jingūmae (exit 5); Ⓡ JR Yamanote line to Harajuku (Omote-sandō exit)

The Apartment Café is a good afternoon refuge for snacks like pasta or spring rolls, but in the evenings it transforms into more of a cocktail lounge where you can spend a low-key evening among locals.

⭐ PLAY
⭐ CROCODILE クロコダイル *Live music*

☎ 3499 5205; B1F, New Sekiguchi Bldg, 6-18-8 Jingūmae, Shibuya-ku; cover from ¥2000; ⏰ 6pm-2am; ⓜ Chiyoda line to Meiji-jingūmae (exit 4)

In Harajuku along Meiji-dōri, Crocodile has live music seven nights a week. It's a spacious place with lots of room for dancing if the music moves you. Tunes cover the gamut from jazz to reggae or rock-and-roll. The cover charge includes one drink.

★ JINGŪ STADIUM 神宮球場
Spectator sports
☎ 3404 8999; 1-13 Kasumigaokamachi, Shinjuku-ku; tickets from ¥1500;
Ⓖ Ginza line to Gaienmae (north exit)
Jingū Baseball Stadium was originally built to host the 1964 Olympics and is where the Yakult Swallows are based. Baseball season runs from April through to the end of October; check the *Japan Times* to see who's playing.

★ NATIONAL STADIUM
国立競技場 *Spectator sports*
☎ 3403 1151; 1-15 Kasumigaokamachi, Shinjuku-ku; tickets from ¥2000; Ⓖ Toei Ōedo line to Kokuritsu Kyōgijō (exit A2);
Ⓡ Chūō line to Sendagaya (east exit)

J-League soccer is booming in Japan, though nay-sayers had predicted its rapid decline with the departure of the 2002 World Cup (awarded to Japan, jointly with Korea). The increased interest in the game has remained, and the Japanese have embraced it almost as enthusiastically as baseball.

★ TOKYO METROPOLITAN GYMNASIUM 東京体育館
Sports & recreation
☎ 5474 2111; www.tef.or.jp/tmg /index.php; 1-17-1 Sendagaya, Shibuya-ku; pool/gym for 2 hrs ¥600/450; ⏱ 9am-11pm Mon-Fri, 9am-10pm Sat, 9am-9pm Sun;
Ⓡ Chūō & Sōbu lines to Sendagaya (main exit), Ⓖ Toei Ōedo line to Kokuritsu Kyōgijō (exits A4 & A5)
Easily accessed and with comprehensive facilities that include two swimming pools, this spaceshiplike structure is just across the street from Sendagaya Station.

>SHIBUYA

Urban anthropologists will find much of interest in the field here in Shibuya, ground zero for Tokyo youth culture. You've probably seen scenes of Shibuya Crossing before, with the flood of humanity that the green light unleashes every few minutes, beneath the moving screens on buildings towering overhead. Shibuya department stores cater to the turnover of trends consumed by the subcultures cruising the street in packs. The more head-turning tribes include (but are certainly not limited to) *mamba,* the girls with the deep, fake tans, white eye makeup and bleached-blonde hair, who are usually decked out in microminis and tall boots. The *mamba* make up only a subset of *gyaru* (gal) culture, which is driven by consumerism, fashion and Shibuya-kei (Shibuya type) music. *Gyaru* culture splits into other variations, much like the alleys snaking off Shibuya Crossing – and these alleys form their natural habitat. You'll find them in its all-you-can-eat dessert cafés, specialised record shops, *izakaya* (pubs-eateries) and clubs, discount shops selling accessories and a million boutiques selling the look of the moment.

SHIBUYA

👁 SEE

👁 HACHIKŌ STATUE
ハチ公像

Outside the Hachikō exit of the Shibuya JR station is that exit's namesake and most famous meeting spot: the Hachikō statue (below). While the story behind it is poignant, its function as a meeting place is logical.

👁 LOVE HOTEL HILL

Around the top of Dōgenzaka is the highest concentration of love hotels in Tokyo. While ostensibly a place for amorous couples, keep it in mind as a good place to crash if you're out late clubbing in the area; rates are pretty reasonable for overnight stays (see opposite).

👁 PARCO FACTORY
パルコファクトリー

☎ 3477 5873; www.parco-art.com; 6F, Parco Part 1, 15-1 Udagawachō, Shibuya-ku; admission; ⏰ 10am-9pm; 🚃 JR Yamanote line to Shibuya (Hachikō exit)

WORTH THE TRIP

The **Hara Museum of Contemporary Art** (☎ 3445 0651; www.haramuseum.or.jp; 4-7-25 Kita-Shinagawa, Shinagawa-ku, admission ¥700; ⏰ 11am-5pm Tue & Thu, Sat & Sun, 11am-8pm Wed; 🚃 JR Yamanote line to Shinagawa, Takanawa exit) is an excellent, adventurous museum that showcases contemporary art by local and international avant-garde artists. As well as exhibiting works by the likes of Gilbert & George (UK) and Cindy Sherman (US), the museum sponsors excellent workshops and presentations by those visiting artists. It's a 15-minute walk from Shinagawa Station; there's a good map on the website.

In line with the neighbourhood vibe, this gallery favours contemporary art with a pop-culture flavour. Recent exhibitions have included a retrospective of *otaku* god Bome's figure sculptures, works inspired by the deceased 'Father of Anime' Osamu Tezuka and a toy exhibition.

A DOG'S LIFE

In the 1920s a professor who taught at what is now Tokyo University kept a small Akita dog named Hachikō. Hachikō accompanied the professor to Shibuya Station every morning, then returned in the afternoons to await the professor's arrival. One spring day in 1925, the professor died of a stroke while at the university and never came home. Hachikō continued to turn up at the station daily to wait for his master, until Hachikō's own death 10 years later. The dog's faithfulness touched the locals, who built a statue to honour his memory in the place where he died. Nowadays, Hachikō's statue is a favourite meeting spot, so fittingly, he's usually surrounded by people waiting for their someones.

LOVE HOTELS

These days, Japan's famous love hotels are more politely referred to as 'boutique' or 'fashion' hotels. There's a love hotel for everyone, from miniature Gothic castles to Middle-Eastern temples…and these are just the buildings – some room themes can be even more outrageous. Some hotels are now catering more to Japanese women's tastes (think pink and cute). Although they're most highly concentrated on Love Hotel Hill (opposite), there are love hotels in most districts. Peek into a few of the entrances to check out the screen with illuminated pictures of available rooms; some lobbies even have vending machines selling sex toys. You can stay for a 'rest' of several hours, but if you want to stay overnight, check-in is usually after 9pm or 10pm and the rates are fairly inexpensive (around ¥8000). Same-sex couples might have trouble checking in, but insisting that you're *tomodachi* (friends) may get you in.

◉ TEPCO ELECTRIC ENERGY MUSEUM 電力館

☎ 3477 1191; 1-12-10 Jinnan, Shibuya-ku; admission free; ☷ 10am-6pm Thu-Tue; ⓡ JR Yamanote line to Shibuya (Hachikō exit); ⓓ ⓧ ⓧ

This is one of Tokyo's better science museums, offering seven floors of dynamic exhibitions on every conceivable aspect of electricity and its production. There are innumerable hands-on displays and an excellent, free English handout that explains everything.

◉ TOBACCO & SALT MUSEUM たばこと塩の博物館

☎ 3476 2041; 1-16-8 Jinnan, Shibuya-ku; admission ¥100/50; ☷ 10am-6pm Tue-Sun; ⓡ JR Yamanote line to Shibuya (Hachikō exit)

This unusual little museum has detailed exhibits on the labour-intensive methods of salt produc-

tion practised in premodern Japan. On the tobacco topic, find vintage lighters, cigarette packs and advertisements illustrating the history of tobacco. While there's little English signage, much of the material is self-explanatory.

⬛ SHOP

There must be a hundred record shops in Udagawachō alone, many focusing on one genre of music. Their stacks usually include rare vinyl, releases available in Japan only and the standard fare you would expect to find in that reggae/Motown/fill-in-the-blank specialist.

▣ AND A *Fashion*

☎ 5428 6720; www.&-a.com; 1-3-4 Jinnan, Shibuya-ku; ☷ 10am-6pm; ⓡ JR Yamanote line to Shibuya (Hachikō exit)

Worth a look for its mix of jewellery, wallets and the like.

☐ DISK UNION
ディスクユニオン *Music*

☎ 3476 2627; http://diskunion.net in Japanese; 30-7 Udagawachō, Shibuya-ku; ☙ 11.30am-9pm; 🚇 JR Yamanote line to Shibuya (Hachikō exit)

The Disk Union chain sells used and new records here at its location on Center-gai. Each floor specialises in a different genre, including punk and jazz. There's another large branch in Shinjuku (p93) and smaller outposts elsewhere in Tokyo.

☐ LOFT ロフト
Homewares & novelties

☎ 3462 3807; 21-1 Udagawachō, Shibuya-ku; ☙ 10am-9pm; 🚇 JR Yamanote line to Shibuya (Hachikō exit)

Insert expendable income here. Loft offers an enormous range of useful goodies such as silk washcloths, sleek furniture and brightly coloured kitchenware, but the best merchandise is the goofier stuff, such as shoe fresheners shaped like smiley-faced hedgehogs, mobile-phone charms and other seductive silliness. It has another branch in Ikebukuro (p86).

☐ MANDARAKE まんだらけ
Books

☎ 3477 0777; www.mandarake.co.jp; B2F, Shibuya Beam Bldg, 31-2 Udagawachō, Shibuya-ku; ☙ noon-8pm; 🚇 JR Yamanote line to Shibuya (Hachikō exit)

The Shibuya branch of Mandarake stocks a range of new manga and also boasts performances by real, live *cosplay* (costume-play) kids in full-on *anime* character drag. Avid fans should also make the trek to Mandarake's huge flagship store in Nakano, with three floors packed with all manner of new and used manga, *anime*, games and character-related collectibles.

☐ MANHATTAN RECORDS
マンハッタンレコード
Music

☎ 3477 7737; 1F, 10-1 Udagawachō, Shibuya-ku; ☙ noon-9pm; 🚇 JR Yamanote line to Shibuya (Hachikō exit)

Rifle through the records in Manhattan for hip-hop and a look at the flyers for local club schedules. There's also a cluster of record shops down the alleys on either side of the Manhattan building, so shop around a bit.

☐ PARCO 1, 2 & 3
パルコパート1, 2&3
Department store

☎ 3464 5111; 15-1 Udagawachō, Shibuya-ku; ☙ 10am-8.30pm; 🚇 JR Yamanote line to Shibuya (Hachikō exit)

If you see it strutting across Shibuya Crossing, you'll find some version of it at Parco parts 1, 2 and 3. These interconnected department stores are mostly targeted toward fans of Vivienne Westwood and to other designers

THE OTAKU ONUS

Much in the way that the innocuous French word *avec* (literally meaning 'with') has been co-opted by the Japanese to mean 'together as a couple', the word *otaku* has in recent years become lingo for 'nerd' or 'geek' outside of Japan, mostly in reference to and used among the manga or gamer ilk.

In Japan, though *otaku* can colloquially mean 'geek', the many layers of its meaning make it a loaded word to be used very selectively. The original translation of the word is an obscure honorific for 'your house', which developed into code for 'you' among, well, nerds with a common obsessive interest in manga and a degree of social discomfort. Eventually the word *otaku* became associated in popular culture with socially maladapted shut-ins and those many related negative connotations.

Unless you're pretty certain you're among peers, use with discretion.

favouring the schoolgirl look. They also have art galleries that feature multimedia installations, avant-garde painting and fashion-oriented exhibitions.

🏠 RAGTAG *Fashion*
☎ 3476 6848; www.ragtag.jp; 1-17-7 Jinnan, Shibuya-ku; ⏰ noon-9pm; 🚇 JR Yamanote line to Shibuya (Hachikō exit)

Hitting the secondhand shops of Tokyo is a great strategy for your wallet not to take such a hit. Ragtag is one reliable source for upmarket finds, particularly for Japanese-designer labels, for both men and women.

🏠 RECOFAN レコファン
Music
☎ 5454 0161; www.recofan.co.jp; 4F, Shibuya Beam Bldg, 31-2 Udagawachō, Shibuya-ku; ⏰ 11.30am-9pm; 🚇 JR Yamanote line to Shibuya (Hachikō exit)

With several branches around town, this arm of Recofan stocks a wide variety of music, including folk, soul, J-pop and reggae. Between this store and the Mandarake (opposite) shop in the basement, you could lose several hours in here.

🏠 SHIBUYA 109 渋谷１０９
Department store
☎ 3477 5111; 2-29-1 Dōgenzaka, Shibuya-ku; ⏰ 10am-9pm Mon-Fri, 11am-10.30pm Sat & Sun; 🚇 JR Yamanote line to Shibuya (Hachikō exit)

Shibuya 109 is the department store selling the trends *du jour* of Shibuya's youth culture, whether it's the minidresses in blindingly saturated colours for the *gyaru* set or the bunched-up ankle socks the schoolgirls are so fond of pairing with their tiny skirts.

🏠 THREE MINUTES HAPPINESS
Homewares & novelties

☎ 5459 1851; 3-5 Udagawachō, Shibuya-ku; ⏱ 11am-9pm; 🚇 JR Yamanote line to Shibuya (Hachikō exit)
Three minutes' worth is guaranteed, but your mileage may vary. This discount shop sells clothes out of decommissioned grocery-store freezers, and makes the shopping experience fun as well as cheap. Downstairs are clothes, shoes and accessories, while lurking upstairs are inexpensive homewares and kitchen knick-knacks.

🏠 TŌKYŪ HANDS
東急ハンズ
Homewares & novelties

☎ 5489 5111; 12-18 Udagawachō, Shibuya-ku; ⏱ 10am-8.30pm; 🚇 JR Yamanote line to Shibuya (Hachikō exit)
Although this branch is a little more cramped than the one at Takashimaya Times Square, this detracts not at all from the appeal of the wonderful wares. Other stores can be found in Shinjuku (p94) and Ikebukuro (p86).

🏠 TOWER RECORDS
タワーレコード *Music*

☎ 3496 3661; 7F, Tower Records Bldg, 1-22-14 Jinnan, Shibuya-ku; ⏱ 10am-11pm; 🚇 JR Yamanote line to Shibuya (Hachikō exit)
Yep, it's a chain, but this Tower is Tokyo's largest music store. Despite its size, this place gets packed.

Shop for shark suits and novelties at Tōkyū Hands

Tower also carries a large selection of English-language books and an extensive array of magazines and newspapers from around the world. Magazines here are considerably cheaper than elsewhere around town.

🍴 EAT

🍴 DEN ROKUEN-TEI
デンロクエンテイ
Asian fusion　　　　　　　¥¥

☎ 6415 5489; 8F, Parco Part 1, 15-1 Udagawacho, Shibuya-ku; ⏱ 11am-midnight; 🚇 JR Yamanote line to Shibuya (Hachikō exit)
Modern twists on seasonally changing Japanese *izakaya* dishes are matched with an array of wine,

beer and sake cocktails. Private tatami (woven floor matting) rooms are available, but at this relaxed, stylish perch on the top of Parco 1, the lovely open-air terrace is the prime property.

🍴 KAIKAYA 開花屋
Izakaya   ¥¥

☎ 3770 0878; www.kaikaya.com; 23-7 Maruyamachō, Shibuya-ku; ⏱ 11.30am-3pm & 5-11pm Mon-Fri, 11.30am-11pm Sat; 🚇 Keiō Inokashira line to Shinsen (main exit) 🚇 JR Yamanote line to Shibuya (Hachikō exit)

This friendly *izakaya* is a little tricky to find, but once you're there you'll be rewarded by its friendly atmosphere and excellent, seasonal fish dishes that use fusion elements without losing too much of the food's essential Japanese strengths. Also, happily, this place has an English menu. Walking along Dōgenzaka away from Shibuya station, turn right at the police box and ask for directions.

🍴 KANTIPUR
カンティプール
Nepalese   ¥¥

☎ 3770 5358; B1F, 16-6 Sakuragaokachō, Shibuya-ku; ⏱ 11.30am-3pm & 5-11pm; 🚇 JR Yamanote line to Shibuya (south exit); Ⓥ

Happily for vegetarians, this Nepalese restaurant has a broad range of acceptable edibles, and the portions of curries and tandoori

dishes are large. Kantipur is in the basement of its building, whose entrance is marked by the brightly coloured signs on the street.

🍴 SAKANA-TEI 酒菜亭
Izakaya   ¥¥

☎ 3780 1313; 4th fl, Koike Bldg, 2-23-15 Dōgenzaka, Shibuya-ku; ⏱ 5.30-11pm Mon-Sat; 🚇 JR Yamanote line to Shibuya (Hachikō exit)

This unpretentious but slightly posh *izakaya* is a sake specialist much sought after by connoisseurs, and is good value for the quality. Though there's no English menu, you can point to dishes displayed on the counter, and start with a sampler set of sake. Call ahead for reservations, but turn off your mobile phone once you're in – house rules.

🍴 SONOMA ソノマ
American   ¥¥

☎ 3462 7766; www.sonomatokyo.com; 2-25-17 Dōgenzaka, Shibuya-ku; ⏱ 6-11.30pm Mon-Thu, 6pm-midnight Fri & Sat; 🚇 JR Yamanote line to Shibuya (Hachikō exit); ♿ Ⓥ

Sonoma's well-balanced menu of California cuisine is further enhanced by a warm, well-lit space. Mains on offer include pork chops with apples, brown sugar and sage, and pan-seared salmon with herb risotto. Dinner here gains free entry to the Ruby Room (p128) upstairs, a fitting place for all-night drinking.

NEIGHBOURHOODS

SHIBUYA

🍴 TORIYOSHI 鳥良
Yakitori   ¥¥

☎ 5784 3373; B1F Sekaido Bldg, 2-10-10 Dōgenzaka, Shibuya-ku; 🕙 5pm-midnight Mon-Thu, 5pm-4am Fri & Sat; 🚇 JR Yamanote line to Shibuya (Hachikō exit)

Toriyoshi does *yakitori* (skewers of grilled chicken) stepped up a notch in sophistication, pairing it with wine and cocktails without sacrificing its earthy, charcoal-grilled appeal. Set dinners are a good way to try a variety of *yakitori* and tofu.

🍸 DRINK

🍸 BELGO ベルゴ *Bar*

☎ 3409 4442; B1F, 3-18-7 Shibuya, Shibuya-ku; 🕙 5.30pm-2am Mon-Thu & Sat, 5.30pm-4.30am Fri, 4pm-midnight Sun; 🚇 JR Yamanote line to Shibuya (south exit)

If you're into Belgian beer, have we got a bar for you. Pouring over 100 kinds of beer, including Guinness and Chimay on draught, Belgo rounds out its liquid offerings with quality Euro-style pub fare like classic fish and chips.

🍸 DOMA DOMA 土間土間
Izakaya

☎ 5728 1099; B1F, Minagawa Bldg, 1-22-10 Jinnan, Shibuya-ku; 🕙 5pm-5am; 🚇 JR Yamanote line to Shibuya (Hachikō exit)

This is an easy-to-find *izakaya* along Jingū-dōri, serving a younger crowd than the salarymen boozing

it up at its Shinjuku counterparts. Order a pitcher of *nama biiru* (draught beer) and a few Japanese dishes off the picture menu, but beware of the more fusion-style offerings that are less hit and more miss.

🍸 INSOMNIA LOUNGE インソムニアラウンジ
Lounge

☎ 3476 2735; B1F; Kushin Bldg, 26-5 Udagawachō, Shibuya-ku; 🕙 6pm-5am; 🚇 JR Yamanote line to Shibuya (Hachikō exit)

Red is the colour of Insomnia. Mirrored by reflective surfaces all around you, your red-eye will blend right into the ruby interior of this laid-back lounge. It doesn't promise any miracle cures for insomniacs but will keep the sleepless going 'til dawn with a good mix of music, cocktails and decent food.

🍸 PINK COW ピンクカウ
Bar

☎ 3406 5597; www.thepinkcow.com; B1F, Villa Moderna, 1-3-18 Shibuya, Shibuya-ku; 🕙 5pm-late Tue-Sun; 🚇 JR Yamanote line to Shibuya (Hachikō exit)

The Pink Cow is a funky, sociable place where something's always going on – local artwork adorns the walls, live music happens, and the place hosts gatherings of venture-capital seekers to stitch-and-bitchers (knitting groups) alike. There's often a cover charge for a special event. Come for the terrific all-you-can-eat buffet (¥2800) every Friday and Saturday evening, and mingle with an international crowd.

⭐ PLAY

⭐ BUNKAMURA THEATRE COCOON
文化村シアターコクーン
Theatre

☎ 3477 9111; www.bunkamura.co.jp/english; 2-24-1 Dōgenzaka, Shibuya-ku; tickets from ¥4000; ⏱ 10am-7pm Sun-Thu, 10am-9pm Fri & Sat; 🚃 JR Yamanote line to Shibuya (Hachikō exit); ♿

Bunkamura, a behemoth of an arts centre, houses a cinema, theatre, concert hall and art gallery. Theatre Cocoon provides an intimate space for musical and theatrical performances from a variety of backgrounds, from the innovative to the offbeat traditional. Check the website for info on current productions.

⭐ CINE AMUSE EAST & WEST
シネアミューズ *Cinema*

☎ 3496 2888; 2-23-12 Dōgenzaka, Shibuya-ku; tickets ¥1800/1000, ¥1000 on 1st day of month (except Jan); ⏱ 10am-11pm; 🚃 JR Yamanote line to Shibuya (Hachikō exit)

Equipped with two screens and an excellent sound system, Cine Amuse has regular screenings

of Japanese movies subtitled in English, as well as international releases. It's a small but comfy space, and well placed for post-cinema amusement in Shibuya.

⭐ CINEMA RISE
シネマライズ *Cinema*

☎ 3464 0051; 13-17 Udagawachō; tickets ¥1800/1000, ¥1000 on 1st day of month (except Jan); ⏱ 10am-11pm; 🚃 JR Yamanote line to Shibuya (Hachikō exit)

Quality independent films are what you'll catch at Cinema Rise, another cinema in the heart of Shibuya.

⭐ CLUB ASIA クラブアジア
Club

☎ 5458 2551; www.clubasia.co.jp in Japanese; 1-8 Maruyamachō, Shibuya-ku; cover around ¥2500; ⏱ 5pm-5am; 🚃 JR Yamanote line to Shibuya (Hachikō exit)

This massive techno/soul club is worth a visit if you're on the younger end of 20-something. Events here are usually jam-packed every night. If you need some fuel to burn on the dance floor, they have a restaurant serving Southeast Asian food until 10pm.

⭐ CLUB QUATTRO
クラブクアトロ *Live music*

☎ 3477 8750; www.club-quattro.com/schedule_shib.php in Japanese; 4F & 5F, Parco Quattro Bldg, 32-13 Udagawachō, Shibuya-ku; cover varies; ⏱ 6pm-late; 🚃 JR Yamanote line to Shibuya (Hachikō exit)

Club Quattro is an established showcase venue for local and international rockers. It's actually in one of the Parco department store buildings (Parco Quattro), which makes for a slightly odd entry. Be sure to buy tickets in advance.

⭐ HARLEM *Club*

☎ 3461 8806; www.harlem.co.jp; 2F & 3F, Dr Jeekahn's Bldg, 2-4 Maruyamachō, Shibuya-ku; cover ¥2000-3000; ◷ 10pm-5am Tue-Sat; 🚇 JR Yamanote line to Shibuya (Hachikō exit)

On the 2nd and 3rd floor of the Dr Jeekahn's Building, this club is where Tokyo B-boys and B-girls come for soul and hip-hop spun by international DJs. Harlem maintains a policy of not admitting groups of foreign males, so guys, come with a girlfriend.

⭐ JZ BRAT *Live music*

☎ 5728 0168; www.jzbrat.com in Japanese; 2F, Cerulean Tower Tōkyū Hotel, 26-1 Sakuragaokachō, Shibuya-ku; cover varies; ◷ from 6pm Mon-Sat; 🚇 JR Yamanote line to Shibuya (south exit)

This sleek jazz club is an intimate venue with a sophisticated vibe, hosting performances not limited solely to jazz, though even the jazz ranges from solo vocalists to improvisational trios. Touring performers of folk and electronica also pass through; check local listings to find out what's on.

⭐ KANZE NŌ-GAKUDŌ
観世能楽堂 *Theatre*

☎ 3469 5241; 1-16-4 Shōtō, Shibuya-ku; tickets from ¥3000; ◷ times vary; 🚇 JR Yamanote line to Shibuya (Hachikō exit)

This theatre is associated with one of the oldest and most highly respected schools of *nō* (classical Japanese musical drama) in Tokyo. By far the most exciting performances are the occasional outdoor night ones of Takigi Nō, where the masked actors are illuminated by huge burning torches. It's a transporting experience, only a 15-minute walk from Shibuya station.

⭐ LA.MAMA ラママ
Live music

☎ 3464 0801; www.lamama.net in Japanese; B1F, Primera Dogenzaka Bldg, 1-15-3 Dōgenzaka, Shibuya-ku; cover from ¥2000; ◷ 6pm-late; 🚇 JR Yamanote line to Shibuya (Hachikō exit)

For a dose of current local-centric music, La.mama is a good bet for catching live, mainstream Japanese acts. The room is fairly spacious, but even when the place gets crowded you'll be close enough to get be-sweated by the next rising star out of Tokyo.

⭐ RUBY ROOM ルビルーム
Lounge

☎ 3780 3022; www.rubyroomtokyo.com; 2F, Kasumi Bldg, 2-25-17 Dōgenzaka, Shibuya-ku; cover ¥2000; ◷ 9pm-late; 🚇 JR Yamanote line to Shibuya (Hachikō exit)

This cool, sparkly gem of a cocktail lounge is on the hill behind the 109 Building. With both DJed and live music, the Ruby Room is an appealing spot for older kids hanging in Shibuya. The cover includes one drink, but if you dine downstairs at Sonoma, admission is free. There's a simple map with directions on their website.

⭐ SHIBUYA O-EAST
渋谷オーイースト
Live music

☎ 5458 4681; www.shibuya-o.com; 2-14-8 Dōgenzaka, Shibuya-ku; cover from ¥2500; 🕐 7pm-late; 🚇 JR Yamanote line to Shibuya (Hachikō exit)

One of an empire of 'O' clubs on Love Hotel Hill, O-East is the most massive, playing host to well-known Japanese and international performers. You'll need to book ahead, as this is a popular place that tends to sell out.

⭐ SHIBUYA O-WEST
渋谷オーウエスト
Live music

☎ 5784 7088; www.shibuya-o.com; 2-3 Maruyamachō, Shibuya-ku; cover from ¥2500; 🕐 7pm-late; 🚇 JR Yamanote line to Shibuya (Hachikō exit)

Another outpost in the 'O' empire of Shibuya TV, O-West is just across the street from its eastern counterpart and tends more towards punk rock and J-pop.

As with its sister club, reserve your tickets in advance.

⭐ TOKYO METROPOLITAN CHILDREN'S HALL
東京都児童会館
Amusement park

☎ 3409 6361; www.fukushihoken .metro.tokyo.jp/jidou/English/index.html; 1-18-24 Shibuya, Shibuya-ku; admission free; 🕐 9am-5pm; 🚇 JR Yamanote line to Shibuya (Hachikō exit)

This place has six floors of fun activities for children, and best of all, it's free! On weekends, the rooftop playground is open for romping around. But every day, there are age-appropriate art projects, storytelling and music-making, and lots of creative indoor play areas.

⭐ WOMB ウーム *Club*

☎ 5459 0039; www.womb.co.jp in Japanese; 2-16 Maruyama-chō, Shibuya-ku; cover ¥1500-4000; 🕐 8pm-late; 🚇 JR Yamanote line to Shibuya (Hachikō exit)

'Oomu' (as pronounced by the Japanese) is all house, techno and drum 'n' bass. The four floors of this place get jammed on weekends. Check Shibuya record shops to pick up a flyer beforehand, or print one from the website, and they'll knock ¥500 to ¥1000 off the cover. Photo ID required at the door.

>EBISU & DAIKANYAMA

Ebisu and Daikanyama don't offer much in the way of spectacular sights, but for a relaxed walk in a hip, low-key area, they exude an effortlessly stylish air. At the southern terminus of the Ebisu Skywalk (a moving walkway) is Yebisu Garden Place, an ersatz Euro-style shopping and entertainment complex surrounding a large courtyard. Apart from the usual restaurants and boutiques, there's also a beer museum and a marvellous photography museum.

To the north of Ebisu station, Daikanyama is one of Tokyo's upscale neighbourhoods with an artsy leaning, where the streets have a more European feel. Fashion here is aimed towards a young yet upscale demographic that has lost none of its edge while pumping up the sophistication. Shops in the Daikanyama alleys offer styles from established international designers to independent locals, while outdoor café culture thrives here. Design fiends will feel right at home here.

EBISU & DAIKANYAMA

A **B** **C** **D**

1

Sarugakuchō
猿楽町

Meiji-dori

Hiro-o

16

Daikanyama
代官山

Hirō
広尾

8

Ebisu
Prime
Square
Plaza

19

2

Hachiman-dori

Daikanyama
Address

● Post
Office

Daikanyama

14

6

13

Ebisu
higashi
kōen

Hibiya Line

Shibuya-gawa

18

22

12

Ebisu

20

Ebisu-
Nishi

10

15

Ebisu

Ebisu
恵比寿

Gaien-nishi-dori

9

3

Matsuzakaya

Ebisu-
Minami
恵比寿南

Skywalk

Naka-
Meguro
中目黒

Ebisu-
minami kōen
恵比寿南公園

America-bashi

Yebisu
Garden Pl

1

2

Taillevent
Robuchon

4

Ebisu View
Tower

Shuto Expwy No 2
首都高速2号

4

Yamate-dori 山手通り

Mita
三田

Chaya-zaka (slope)

Meguro-ku
目黒区

Meguro-gawa

3

Shizen
Kyōiku-en
自然教育園

5

Tokyo Metropolitan
Teien Art Museum

Shinagawa-ku
品川区

17

Meguro

Meguro

Gonnosuke Zaka

6

Meguro-dori

2

Meguro-dori

Shimo-
Meguro
下目黒

Kami-
Ōsaki
上大崎

◉ SEE

◉ BEER MUSEUM YEBISU
恵比寿麦酒記念館
☎ 5423 7255; www.sapporobeer.jp
/english/guide/yebisu; 4-20-1 Ebisu,
Shibuya-ku; admission free; ⏲ 10am-6pm
Tue-Sun; ⊠ JR Yamanote line to Ebisu
(east exit to Skywalk)
Run by Sapporo Breweries,
this museum has lots of good
exhibits on the brewing process,
but the real pull is the Tasting
Lounge, where you can kick back
and sample Sapporo's various
limited-edition brews. Sorry, no
freebies here – it's ¥200 per glass
or ¥400 for a sampler of four –
but that's still quite a deal.

◉ MEGURO PARASITOLOGICAL MUSEUM
目黒寄生虫館
☎ 3716 1264; http://kiseichu.org
/english.aspx; 4-1-1 Shimo-Meguro,
Meguro-ku; admission free; ⏲ 10am-5pm
Tue-Sun; ⊠ JR Yamanote line to Meguro
(west exit); ☒ ☒
Some people will *not* find exhibits
like the 9m-long tapeworm to
their liking, but for others, this
tiny museum is gruesomely
fascinating. Though there isn't
much English signage, kids will
get a kick out of the rows of
formaldehyde-preserved critters,
which are labelled with their Latin
names. Upstairs, the gift counter
sells parasite-themed keychains
and T-shirts.

◉ NATIONAL INSTITUTE FOR NATURE STUDY
国立自然教育園
☎ 3441 7176; www.ins.kahaku.go.jp
/english/english.html; 5-21-5
Shirokanedai, Minato-ku; admission
¥300/free; ⏲ 9am-4.30pm Sep-Apr,
9am-5pm May-Aug; ⊠ JR Yamanote line
to Meguro (east exit), ◉ Namboku line to
Shirokanedai (exit 1); ☒ ☒
Prosaic in name but perfect in
nature, this garden (known as Shizen Kyōiku-en in Japanese) is one
of Tokyo's least known and most
appealing getaways. It preserves
the city's original flora in undisci-
plined profusion. Take a walk on
Tokyo's wild side through woods
and swamps, in this haven for
bird-watchers, botanists and those
overdosing on urban rhythms.

◉ TOKYO METROPOLITAN MUSEUM OF PHOTOGRAPHY
東京都写真美術館
☎ 3280 0099; www.syabi.com; 1-13-3
Mita, Meguro-ku; admission varies;
⏲ 10am-6pm Tue, Wed, Sat& Sun,
10am-8pm Thu & Fri; ⊠ JR Yamanote
line to Ebisu (east exit to Skywalk)
Japan's first large-scale museum
devoted entirely to photography,
this wonderfully curated space is
comprised of several galleries. The
emphasis is on Japanese photo-

Shop in Euro-style amid the charming green spaces of Yebisu Garden Place

graphy, but international work is also well represented. As you enter Yebisu Garden Place, the museum is at the very back, towards the right.

SHOP

EVISU TAILOR
エビスヤテーラー *Fashion*

☎ 3710 1999; www.evisu.com; 1-1-5 Kami-Meguro, Meguro-ku; 🕙 11am-8pm; Ⓗ Hibiya line to Naka-meguro

In the early '90s the detail-obsessed founder of Evisu began producing jeans the old-fashioned way, using rescued looms and weaving methods, helping to spawn the Japanese selvedge-denim craze. At Evisu Tai or you can choose the pair you want and have the Evisu logo custom-painted on, or discreet denim-wearers can opt to go logoless.

HACKNET
ハックネット *Books*

☎ 5728 6611; www.hacknet.tv in Japanese; 1-30-10 Ebisu-Nishi, Shibuya-ku; 🕙 11am-8pm; ℝ JR Yamanote line to Ebisu (west exit)

Hacknet, a tiny shop with tall shelves, is a haven for art and design junkies, full of absorbing design porn (we mean it metaphorically) in Ebisu's Q-Flagship Building.

⬠ KAMAWANU かまわぬ
Handicrafts

☎ 3780 0182; www.kamawanu.co.jp
in Japanese; 23-1 Sarugakuchō, Shibuya-ku; ⏱ 11am-7pm; 🚇 JR Yamanote line to Ebisu (west exit) or Tōkyū Tōyoko line to Daikanyama (main exit)

This little shop in Daikanyama specialises in beautifully dyed *tenugui*, those ubiquitous Japanese hand towels that you can fold on your head at the *sentō* (public baths), use to genteelly pat the sweat off the back of your neck on the JR platform, or wrap your *bentō* (boxed meal) in to take with you for lunch. Colourful designs incorporate traditional abstract patterns and representations of natural elements.

⬠ LIMI FEU リミフゥ
Fashion

☎ 3463 6324; www.limifeu.com; 7-4 Daikanyamachō, Shibuya-ku; ⏱ noon-9pm; 🚇 Tōkyū Tōyoko line to Daikanyama

Though she changed her surname from her famous father's (Yohji Yamamoto, that is), his deconstructionist influence certainly informs her designs. At the same time, Limi Feu has created her own distinct, streetwise style that appeals to women with a Daikanyama aesthetic.

⬠ RESTORE *Fashion*

☎ 5768 9877; 3-2-2 Ebisu-Minami, Shibuya-ku; ⏱ noon-8pm; 🚇 JR Yamanote line to Ebisu (west exit), 🚇 Hibiya line to Ebisu (exit 5)

This small but selective second-hand shop along Komazawa-dōri is stocked with middleweight vintage as well as last-year's look. APC and Yohji Yamamoto rub shoulders on the hangers here, and they carry both men's and women's garb. Recycle and refresh your wardrobe.

🍴 EAT

🍴 CARDENAS CHARCOAL GRILL *American* ¥¥¥

☎ 5428 0779; 1-12-14 Ebisu-Nishi, Shibuya-ku; ⏱ 11.30am-2pm & 5.30pm-2am Mon-Fri, 5.30pm-2am Sat & Sun; 🚇 JR Yamanote line to Ebisu (west exit)

California cuisine and wine dominate at this stylish Ebisu institution. As the name would imply, omnivores should choose one of the juicy, charcoal-grilled items like the barbecued ribs, or the seasonally available duck. Vegetarians have fewer options here, though salads, pasta dishes and grilled organic veggies round out the menu.

🍴 IPPŪDŌ 一風堂 *Rāmen* ¥

☎ 5420 2225; 1-3-13 Hiroo, Shibuya-ku; ⏱ 11am-4pm; 🚇 JR Yamanote line to Ebisu (east exit), 🚇 Hibiya line to Ebisu (exits 1 & 2); 👶

Nationally famous, this *rāmen* shop specialises in *tonkotsu* (pork broth) noodles. While the *akamaru rāmen* (rich pork broth with red seasoning oil) is tailored towards the Tokyo palate, the *shiromaru* (milder, 'white' pork broth) is pure Kyūshū (grate fresh garlic over it for authenticity). You'll have to queue at peak periods and, as a courtesy, should take no more than 20 minutes to eat, but it's well worth it.

🍴 SAIKI さいき *Izakaya* ¥¥
☎ 3461 3367; 1-7-12 Ebisu-Nishi, Shibuya-ku; ⏰ 5pm-midnight Mon-Fri; 🚇 JR Yamanote line to Ebisu (west exit)

If you're feeling adventurous enough to have the *izakaya* experience complete with a mandatory (and relatively pricey) appetizer set accompanied by a solid language barrier, then bring your humble self to Saiki and order *omakase* (chef's choice). There's no English menu, but the well-established setting is so intimate and the food is so authentically good that you will be duly rewarded for your troubles.

🍴 URA ウラ
International ¥¥
☎ 5489 1117; 1-17-1 Ebisu-Nishi, Shibuya-ku; ⏰ noon-11pm Sun-Thu, noon-4am Fri & Sat; 🚇 JR Yamanote line to Ebisu (west exit)

With such a wealth of little cafés and bistros around Daikanyama, it can be hard to decide whether you want to nibble a scone or indulge in an afternoon cocktail. But this cool, casual spot is inviting day or night, with excellent, mostly French-style dishes and balanced out by well-chosen wines, good espresso and sumptuous desserts.

🍸 DRINK
🍸 ENJOY! HOUSE
エンジョイハウス *Lounge*
☎ 5489 1591; 2F, Kokuto Bldg, 2-9-9 Ebisu-Nishi, Shibuya-ku; ⏰ 1pm-2am Sun & Tue-Thu, 1pm-4am Fri & Sat, closed 1st Sun of each month; 🚇 JR Yamanote line to Ebisu (west exit)

This retro lounge is run by a free-spirited owner who will elevate your mood. The mix here runs from '80s pop to reggae, and the vibe is relaxed. Best of all, there's no cover charge. Enjoy!

🍸 WHAT THE DICKENS
ワットザディケンズ *Pub*
☎ 3780 2099; www.whatthedickens.jp; 4F, Roob 6 Bldg, 1-13-3 Ebisu-Nishi, Shibuya-ku; ⏰ 5pm-late Tue-Sat, 5pm-midnight Sun; 🚇 JR Yamanote line to Ebisu (west exit), 🚇 Hibiya line to Ebisu (exit 2)

One of Tokyo's better British-style pubs, this one has a pleasant, spacious feel, and there's usually a live band in the corner playing good, mellow music. Good tunes, hearty pub food and Guinness on tap – what more could you want?

PLAY

☆ AIR エアー Club

☎ 5784 3386; www.air-tokyo.com; B1F & B2F, Hikawa Bldg, 2-11 Sarugakuchō, Shibuya-ku; 🚉 Tōkyū Tōyoko line to Daikanyama (main exit) or JR Yamanote line to Shibuya (south exit)

DJs spin mostly house here, and the crowd tends to be happy and friendly – though not huge on dancing. Air is in an alley north-west of Hachiman-dōri, south of Shibuya station; there's a decent map on the website. The entrance to the basement is inside the Frames restaurant. Remember to bring your ID.

☆ BLUES ALLEY JAPAN ブルースアレイ日本 Live Music

☎ 5496 4381; www.bluesalley.co.jp in Japanese; B1F, Hotel Wing International, 1-3-4 Meguro, Meguro-ku; cover from ¥3500; ⏰ 2pm-midnight Mon-Sat; 🚉 JR Yamanote line to Meguro (west exit)

The name pretty well sums it up – this is the relaxed little place you want to come if blues is more your speed than hip-hop. Most who

appear here are highly regarded Japanese blues musicians, with the occasional jazz act thrown into the mix for good measure.

☆ LIQUID ROOM リキッドルーム Live music

☎ 5464 0800; www.liquidroom.net; 3-16-6 Higashi, Shibuya-ku; cover from ¥3000; ⏰ 7pm-late; 🚉 JR Yamanote line to Ebisu (east exit)

Some of the world's greatest performers have graced the stage of the Liquid Room, from the Flaming Lips to Linton Kwesi Johnson. This spacious place in Ebisu is an excellent place to see an old favourite or find a new one.

☆ SMASH HITS スマシヒッツ Karaoke

☎ 3444 0432; www.smashhits.jp; B1F, M2 Hiro-o Bldg, 5-2-26 Hiro-o, Shibuya-ku; admission ¥3500; ⏰ 7pm-3am Mon-Sat; 🚇 Hibiya line to Hiro-o (exit B2)

Watch your friends wince as you deafen them with the Sid Vicious version of 'My Way'. Smash Hits provides excruciating fun of the highest order, with 12,000 English-language songs to choose from for your 15 minutes of fame. There's no time limit, and the cover includes two drinks.

☆ UNIT ユニット *Club*

☎ 5459 8630; www.unit-tokyo.com; B1F-B3F, Za House Bldg, 1-34-17 Ebisu-Nishi, Shibuya-ku; cover from ¥3000; ☽ vary; 🚉 Tōkyū Tōyoko line to Daikanyama, ⊕ Hibiya line to Naka-Meguro

This subterranean space contains a restaurant, club and bar on each descending floor. Shows are mostly big-name Japanese DJ events, but live bands also play here. Be sure to bring ID to get in.

☆ YEBISU GARDEN CINEMA 恵比寿ガーデンシネマ
Cinema

☎ 5420 6161; Yebisu Garden Place, 4-20-2 Ebisu, Shibuya-ku; tickets ¥1800/1000, on 1st day of month ¥1000; ☽ 10am-11pm; 🚉 JR Yamanote line to Ebisu (east exit to Skywalk)

At Yebisu Garden Place, where you can have a bite beforehand and a cocktail afterwards, this cinema is a good place to catch a variety of films. Patrons are called into the theatre in groups according to ticket numbers (first come, first served), bypassing the usual mad rush for the best seats.

☆ YOGAJAYA ヨガジャヤ
Sports & recreation

☎ 5734 3622; www.yogajaya.com; 2F, 1-25-11 Ebisu-Nishi, Shibuya-ku; trial class/mat rental ¥1500/300; ☽ 7am-9.30pm Mon-Fri, 11am-7.30pm Sat & Sun

Mainly Hatha, Ashtanga and Sivananda practices; classes in Japanese and English.

>AKASAKA & ROPPONGI

In a very general sense Akasaka and Roppongi can be compartmen-
talised into two distinct districts: business and pleasure. In Akasaka
and nearby Nagatachō, businessfolk and government suits toil away in
service to big machines and political matters. But just down the road in
Roppongi, the business has historically been leisure. For more than half
a century Roppongi has been the place to cut loose and has not always
had such a savoury reputation. Nowadays, it's the least Japanese part of
Japan – but that doesn't mean it's no fun. Nightlife is concentrated here
so intensely that on Saturday nights you may just choke on the phero-
mone cloud hanging above Roppongi Crossing.

And since the minicity of Roppongi Hills made its hugely anticipated
debut in 2003 and the Tokyo Midtown complex opened in 2007, Roppongi has grown into a day-and-night destination, thus ascending
several levels in class and respectability.

AKASAKA & ROPPONGI

👁 SEE
Hie-jinja 1 F2
Mori Art Museum 2 D5
National Art Center
  Tokyo 3 C4
National Diet
  Building 4 F2
New Ōtani Japanese
  Garden 5 E1
Ōkura Shūkokan 6 F4
Sōgetsu Kaikan 7 D2
Suntory Museum
  of Art 8 D4
Tokyo Tower 9 G6

🛍 SHOP
Aoyama Book
  Center 10 D5
Axis Building 11 E5
Japan Sword 12 G4
Kurofune 13 D4
Tolman Collection 14 H6

🍴 EAT
Asterix 15 E3
Erawan 16 E5
Fukuzushi 17 D5
Gonpachi 18 C5
Inakaya ....(see 32)
Kikunoi 19 D3
La Colina ....(see 8)
L'Atelier de
  Joël Robuchon 20 D5
Moti 21 E2
Seryna 22 D4
Sushi-sei 23 E2
Umaya 24 E2

🍸 DRINK
Agave 25 D4
Bernd's Bar 26 E5
Geronimo 27 D4
Heartland ....(see 20)
Mado Lounge ....(see 2)
Maduro 28 C5

⭐ PLAY
Abbey Road 29 D4
Blue Note 30 A5
BuL-Let's 31 C5
Cavern Club 32 D5
Club 328 ....33 C5
Egbok Azabu Oriental
  Clinic 34 E5
El Café Latino 35 E4
Lovenet 36 D4
Muse 37 B5
New Lex-Edo 38 D5
Salsa Sudada 39 D4
STB 139 ....40 D5
SuperDeluxe 41 C5
Toho Cinemas
  Roppongi Hills 42 D5
Ultra Lounge 43 D4

Please see over for map

◉ SEE

◉ HIE-JINJA 日枝神社

☎ 3581 2471; www.hiejinja.net/jinja/english/index.html; 2-10-5 Nagatachō, Chiyoda-ku; admission free; ⏱ dawn-dusk; ◉ Ginza & Namboku lines to Tameike-sannō (exits 5 & 7)

A casualty of WWII bombing, Hie-jinja dates back to 1659 in its present location. Although the shrine isn't a major attraction, the highlight is the walk up, through a 'tunnel' of red *torii* (shrine gate). It's also the site for one of Japan's most spectacular *matsuri* (festivals). Look for the concrete plaza-style entrance on Sotobori-dōri.

◉ MORI ART MUSEUM 森美術館

☎ 5777 8600; www.mori.art.museum; 53F, Mori Tower, Roppongi Hills, 6-10-1 Roppongi, Minato-ku; admission ¥1500; ⏱ 10am-10pm Wed-Mon, 10am-5pm Tue, closed btwn exhibitions; ◉ Hibiya & Toei Ōedo lines to Roppongi (exits 1c & 3)

Past exhibitions at this well-curated contemporary-arts museum have ranged from a comprehensive exhibition of contemporary African art to a huge, walk-through installation by Kusama Yayo. Museum admission also gets you into the spectacular 360-degree city views of Tokyo City View (and vice versa).

◉ NATIONAL ART CENTER TOKYO 国立新美術館

☎ 5777 8600; www.nact.jp; 7-22-2 Roppongi, Minato-ku; admission varies; ⏱ 10am-6pm Wed & Sat-Mon, 10am-8pm Fri; ◉ Chiyoda line to Nogizaka (exit 6), Hibiya & Toei Ōedo lines to Roppongi (exits 4a & 7); ♿

The undulating glass exterior of this new museum (the third point

Get your fill of contemporary art at Mori Art Museum, Roppongi Hills

in the Roppongi Art Triangle) is alone worth a walk-by, and if the current exhibitions don't interest you, the museum shop is a treasure-trove of exquisite gifts.

◯ NATIONAL DIET BUILDING 国会議事堂

☎ 5521 7445; www.sangiin.go.jp; 1-7-1 Nagatachō, Chiyoda-ku; ⏰ 8am-5pm Mon-Fri; ◉ Hanzōmon, Namboku & Yūrakuchō lines to Nagatachō (exit 1) or Marunouchi & Chiyoda lines to Kokkai-gijidōmae (exit 1)

When the Diet is not in session, you can take free 60-minute tours of this government hall, completed in 1936. Its structure was meant to combine the modern

styles of both Asian and European architecture.

◯ NEW OTANI JAPANESE GARDEN ホテルニューオータニ日本庭園

☎ 3265 1111; www.newotani.co.jp/en /group/garden/index.html; admission free; 4-1 Kioi-chō, Chiyoda-ku; ⏰ 6am-10pm; ◉ Ginza & Marunouchi lines to Akasaka-mitsuke (Belle Vie exit) or Hanzōmon & Yūrakuchō lines to Nagatachō (exit 7)

Though the Hotel New Otani's stunning 400-year-old Japanese garden is open to the public, the hotel doesn't make it especially accessible. The easiest way to find it is via the 1st floor of the hotel's Garden Court shopping complex.

For a taste of government life take a tour of the National Diet Building

⊙ ŌKURA SHŪKOKAN
大倉集古館

☎ 3583 0781; www.okura.com/tokyo /info/shukokan.html; 2-10-3 Toranomon, Minato-ku; admission ¥800/500/ free; ⏰ 10am-4.30pm Tue-Sun; ⊙ Hibiya line to Kamiyachō (exit 4b) or Ginza & Namboku lines to Tameike-sannō (exit 13)

Surrounded by a small but well-populated sculpture garden, this museum has an impressive collection of lacquer writing boxes, scrolls, ancient sculptures and several national treasures. The two-storey museum – with a collection that's rotated seasonally – is definitely worth a look if you're on this side of town.

⊙ SŌGETSU KAIKAN
草月会館

☎ 3408 1151; www.sogetsu.or.jp/eng lish/index.html; Sōgetsu Kaikan Bldg, 7-2-21 Akasaka, Minato-ku; ⏰ 10am-5pm Mon-Thu & Sat, 10am-8pm Fri; ⊙ Ginza, Hanzōmon & Toei Ōedo lines to Aoyama-itchōme (exit 4)

The avant-garde Sōgetsu School of Ikebana, whose philosophy is that ikebana (Japanese flower arrangement) can go beyond its traditional roots, offers ikebana classes in English. Stop by the Sōgetsu Kaikan building for a look at current ikebana exhibits or to enquire about classes.

RENDEZVOUS SPOTS EVERYONE KNOWS…
> *Hachikō* statue (p120); Shibuya
> Studio Alta building (p88); Shinjuku
> Mitsukoshi lion (p56); Ginza
> *The Spider* (Maman sculpture; pp8-9); Roppongi
> *Takamori Saigō* statue (p68); Ueno

⊙ SUNTORY MUSEUM OF ART
サントリー美術館

☎ 3479 8600; www.suntory.com /culture-sports/sma/guide/info.html; 9-7-4 Akasaka, Minato-ku; admission ¥1300/1000/free; ⏰ 10am-6pm Sun-Mon, 10am-8pm Wed-Sat; ⊙ Hibiya & Toei Ōedo lines to Roppongi (exit 8)

Forming one of the corners of what's known as the Roppongi Art Triangle (p16), the Suntory Museum takes up residence at Tokyo Midtown, Roppongi's newest development. Its spacious galleries provide a refuge for the museum's collection of Japanese antiques and beautiful, traditional arts and crafts.

⊙ TOKYO TOWER
東京タワー

☎ 3433 5111; www.tokyotower .co.jp/english; 4-2-8 Shiba-kōen, Minato-ku; main observation deck ¥310-820, special observation deck extra ¥350-600; ⏰ 9am-10pm; ⊙ Hibiya line to Kamiyachō (exits 1 & 2); ♿

Although it might play second fiddle to Roppongi Hills'

Watch the city sparkle from Tokyo Tower (p143)

52nd-floor Tokyo City View, Tokyo Tower still affords a great 360-degree view of the city, best appreciated at night. It retains a sort of oldster charm next to the architectural wonders that have succeeded it. Catch live music on the main observatory, Wednesday and Thursday nights.

🛍 SHOP

Roppongi Hills lit up the neighbourhood when it opened as a much-vaunted microcosm within the greater megalopolis. The high-end shops based within the sexy architectural curves of the Hills still do a brisk business, but the smaller development of Tokyo Midtown down the way has established itself as a sophisticated, design-oriented shopping centre. You'll also find small shops around Akasaka and Roppongi selling antiques and handicrafts.

📖 AOYAMA BOOK CENTER
青山ブックセンター
Books
☎ 3479 0479; 6-1-20 Roppongi, Minato-ku; ⏰ 10am-5am Mon-Sat, 10am-10pm Sun, closed 2nd & 3rd Tue each month; Ⓜ Hibiya & Toei Ōedo lines to Roppongi (exit 3)
The beautifully remodelled Roppongi-dōri branch of Aoyama Book Center is a prime spot for night owls, with a great international selection of reads and a carefully chosen collection of foreign art books. There's another branch nearby in the Roppongi Hills West Walk.

🏠 AXIS BUILDING
アクシスビル
Homewares & novelties
☎ 3587 2781; 5-17-1 Roppongi, Minato-ku; ⏰ 11am-7pm Mon-Sat; Ⓜ Hibiya & Toei Ōedo lines to Roppongi (exit 3)
Billed as a design hub, Tokyo Midtown's sheer size overshadows the Axis Building, but not its collection of interior design–oriented

businesses. Housed in the building are 20 or so galleries and retail shops selling fabrics, furniture and art, as well as a couple of lovely restaurants.

JAPAN SWORD 日本刀剣
Art & antiques

☎ 3434 4321; www.japansword.co.jp; 3-8-1 Toranomon, Minato-ku;
🕑 9.30am-6pm Mon-Fri, 9.30am-5pm Sat; 🚇 Ginza line to Toranomon (exit 2)

If *Kill Bill* revived a long-dormant childhood attraction to swords, this highly respected dealer has a beautiful showroom and lots of experience helping foreigners choose the right *katana* (sword) for their taste and budget. Priciest are the macabre *tameshi-giri* blades that have been 'used on humans'.

KUROFUNE 黒船
Art & antiques

☎ 3479 1552; www.kurofuneantiques.com; 7-7-4 Roppongi, Minato-ku;
🕑 10am-6pm Mon-Sat; 🚇 Toei Ōedo line to Roppongi (exit 7)

Kurofune, run for the past quarter-century by a friendly American collector, carries an awesome treasure trove of Japanese antiques. Correspondingly awesome amounts of cash are necessary for acquiring some of these items, such as painstakingly constructed Edo-period *tansu* (Japanese chests of drawers), but serious antique connoisseurs are well advised to have a look.

TOLMAN COLLECTION
Art & antiques

☎ 3434 1300; www.tolmantokyo.com; 2-2-18 Shiba-Daimon, Minato-ku;
🕑 11am-7pm Wed-Mon; 🚇 Toei Asakusa & Toei Ōedo lines to Daimon (exits A3 & A6)

For collectors keen on picking up some contemporary art, this well-established, estimable gallery represents a strong stable of printmakers, both Japanese and foreign. Although the artists exhibit a fairly broad range of styles ranging from abstract to representative, all of the work has a distinctly Japanese feel.

EAT

This being a historically *gaijin-* (foreigner-) heavy neighbourhood, and now home to sprawling Roppongi Hills and Tokyo Midtown, there's a cornucopia of international cuisine, as well as some of Tokyo's best Japanese restaurants. Consequently, dining out tends to be more expensive than in other areas of the city, but the venues also put forth the extra effort to give all five senses a memorable experience of Tokyo.

🍴 ASTERIX アステリックス
French ¥¥

☎ 5561 0980; B1F, 6-3-16 Akasaka, Minato-ku; ⏰ 11.30am-2pm & 6-10pm Mon-Sat; Ⓜ Chiyoda line to Akasaka (exits 6 & 7); 🔥

A French lunch here is a smashing deal, but dinner has its own merits (ie not so rushed, allowing you to linger over your wine). Portions are large but the dining room is tiny, so reservations are advised. The menu is in French, but servers can translate into English if needed.

🍴 ERAWAN エラワン
Thai ¥¥

☎ 3404 5741; 13F, Roi Bldg, 5-5-1 Roppongi, Minato-ku; ⏰ 5.30-11.30pm Mon-Fri & 5-11.30pm Sat & Sun; Ⓜ Hibiya & Toei Ōedo lines to Roppongi (exit 3)

Not a new kid on the block; Erawan serves spicy curries and green papaya salad, in a setting reminiscent of an outdoor Thai café on some southern shore. Except here, you get a glittering urban view from this top-floor dining venue.

🍴 FUKUZUSHI 福鮨
Sushi & sashimi ¥¥¥

☎ 3402 4116; 5-7-8 Roppongi, Minato-ku; ⏰ 11.30am-2pm & 5.30-11pm Mon-Sat; Ⓜ Hibiya & Toei Ōedo lines to Roppongi (exit 3); Ⓥ

Although the atmosphere here is upscale, Fukuzushi is decidedly

more relaxed than some places in Ginza and Tsukiji. The sushi is some of the best in town, the portions are large, and there's even a full cocktail bar. It's in the alley beyond the Hard Rock Café.

🍴 GONPACHI 権八
Izakaya ¥¥

☎ 5771 0170; www.gonpachi.jp; 1-13-11 Nishi-Azabu, Minato-ku; ⏰ 11.30am-5am; Ⓜ Hibiya, Toei Ōedo lines to Roppongi (exit 2); 🔥

The Edo-village décor and festive buzz in the air makes Gonpachi a great place for celebratory dinners, but do you really need a reason to thrill your palate with half-a-dozen exotic and untried Japanese morsels? Upstairs, you can order everything on the menu, plus sushi. Book ahead.

🍴 INAKAYA 田舎家
Robatayaki ¥¥¥¥

☎ 3408 5040; 5-3-4 Roppongi, Minato-ku; ⏰ 5-11pm; Ⓜ Hibiya & Toei Ōedo lines to Roppongi (exit 3)

Inakaya has gained fame as a top-end *robatayaki* (grilled-to-order seafood and meat). It does raucous, bustling, don't-stand-on-ceremony *robatayaki* with gusto. Point at what you'd like to eat and they'll grill it for you and serve it with a boisterous flourish. You'll pay for the privilege and have a rocking good time doing so.

KAISEKI

Kaiseki (elegant, multicourse Japanese meals) grew as a complement to the traditions of the tea ceremony, with a similar ceremonial emphasis on attention to all of the senses during the dining experience. Each course is not only painstakingly prepared to bring out the flavours of the seasonally changing dishes, but also the colours, textures, and smells, which must be carefully presented to be aesthetically pleasing in every way. It's the height of Japanese cuisine and a singular experience. One of the more accessible places in Tokyo to sample *kaiseki* dining is at Kikunoi (below) in Akasaka.

🍴 KIKUNOI 菊乃井

Kaiseki   ¥¥¥¥

☎ 3568 6055; 6-13-8 Akasaka, Minato-ku; 🕐 5-9pm Mon-Sat; ⊙ Chiyoda line to Akasaka (exit 6)

This Kyoto-based *kaiseki* restaurant has built its reputation over three generations, and its national fame has expanded to international recognition after being awarded with two Michelin stars in 2008. Exquisitely prepared seasonal dishes are as beautiful as they are delicious. If you don't speak Japanese, the bonus is that Kikunoi's Chef Murata has also written a book on *kaiseki,* and the staff helpfully uses the book to explain the dishes you are served.

🍴 LA COLINA ラコリナ

Mexican   ¥¥

☎ 5413 0092; www.lacolina.jp; 1F, Tokyo Midtown Garden Terrace, 9-7-4 Akasaka, Minato-ku; 🕐 11am-midnight; ⊙ Hibiya & Toei Ōedo lines to Roppongi (exit 8)

Run by the same people behind the ever-popular Fonda de la Madrugada (p113), La Colina serves refreshingly authentic Mexican food in a stylish, dark corner of Tokyo Midtown. Or settle yourself on the outdoor terrace to enjoy your taco-and-beer set (a shockingly reasonable ¥1470 at lunch).

🍴 L'ATELIER DE JOËL ROBUCHON ラトリエドゥ ジョエルロブション

French   ¥¥¥

☎ 5772 7500; 2F Hillside, Roppongi Hills, 6-10-1 Roppongi, Minato-ku; 🕐 11.30am-2.30pm & 6-10pm; ⊙ Hibiya & Toei Ōedo lines to Roppongi (exits 1c & 3)

Another two-star Michelin standout, L'Atelier is an upscale French diner fashioned after a sushi bar. While the fantastic dishes are not overly fussy, everything is made to order, which can mean long waits in the queue and over your meal – leaving plenty of time for conversation and anticipation.

🍴 MOTI モティ

Indian ¥¥

☎ 3584 6640; 3F, Kinpa Bldg,
2-14-31 Akasaka, Minato-ku;
🕐 11.30am-10pm; ◎ Chiyoda line to
Akasaka (exit 2); Ⓥ ⅙

You'll get the red-carpet treatment at Moti, where some of Tokyo's best Indian food is served up by attentive and friendly staff, in elegant surroundings. The lunch sets are a terrific deal, and this branch serves *dosa* (rice pancakes) and other South Indian specialities. Moti has another branch in Akasaka, one in Roppongi, and several others beyond.

🍴 NATIONAL AZABU SUPERMARKET
ナショナル麻布

International groceries

☎ 3442 3181; 4-5-2 Minami-Azabu,
Minato-ku; 🕐 9am-8pm; ◎ Hibiya line
to Hiro-o (exits 1 & 2)

Posher than posh can be, National Azabu is where the ambassadorial lackeys are sent to stock up on pâté de foie gras and truffles or their Japanese equivalents, *uni* (sea urchins) and *matsutake* (mushrooms). It's also got an awesome selection of imported wines and natural foods and, importantly, has a pharmacy staffed with English speakers.

🍴 SERYNA 瀬里奈

Sukiyaki & shabu-shabu ¥¥¥

☎ 3402 1051; 3-12-2 Roppongi,
Minato-ku; 🕐 noon-11.30pm Mon-Fri,
noon-10.30pm Sat & Sun; ◎ Hibiya & Toei
Ōedo lines to Roppongi (exits 3 & 5); ⅙

Although it feels a bit aged, like the high-quality Kōbe beef that draws expats and visiting guests here, Seryna provides a dignified backdrop for *shabu-shabu*, sukiyaki and *teppanyaki* (table-top grilling). The restaurant surrounds an attractive rock garden.

🍴 SUSHI-SEI 寿司清

Sushi & sashimi ¥¥

☎ 3582 9503; 3-11-14 Akasaka,
Minato-ku; 🕐 11.30am-2pm & 5-
10.30pm Mon-Fri, 11.45am-2pm & 4.30-
10pm Sat; ◎ Ginza & Marunouchi lines
to Akasaka-mitsuke (Belle Vie exit)

Taste top-notch sushi at Sushi-sei, which traces its ancestry back to Tsukiji. Like Akasaka itself, Sushi-sei conducts serious business. Try to hit it during off-peak hours, or expect to queue with hungry government officials and financial movers and shakers.

🍴 UMAYA うまや

Traditional Japanese ¥¥

☎ 6229 1661; 4-2-32 Akasaka, Minato-ku; 🕐 11am-2.30pm & 5pm-midnight
Mon-Thu, 11am-2.30pm & 5pm-1am Fri,
5-11pm Sat; ◎ Ginza & Marunouchi lines
to Akasaka-mitsuke (Belle Vie exit); Ⓥ

This atmospheric, traditionally styled restaurant serves a variety of Japanese dishes, incorporating free-range chicken, house-made tofu and a surprising number of vegetarian dishes (though not so many at lunch). To find it from Hitotsugi-dōri, head for Akasaka-fudōson-jinja but turn left just inside the shrine gate.

☥ DRINK

If, at the end of a long day, you need to unwind in a quiet corner nursing a single-malt Scotch, then the lobbies and high-rise bars of Akasaka hotels will serve nicely. But gearing up for a big night out means starting in Roppongi, where you can drink up for cheap in a dive bar, or kick off your evening with a stylish cocktail.

☥ AGAVE アガヴェ Bar
☎ 3497 0229; B1F, Clover Bldg, 7-15-10 Roppongi, Minato-ku; ⏱ 6.30pm-2am Mon-Thu, 6.30pm-4am Fri & Sat; Ⓜ Hibiya & Toei Ōedo lines to Roppongi (exit 2)

This amiable spot is for those more interested in savouring the subtleties of its 400-plus varieties of tequila than tossing back shots of Cuervo. Sip an *añejo* (aged tequila) or try one of their margaritas.

☥ BERND'S BAR
バーンズバー *Bar*
☎ 5563 9232; www.berndsbar.com; 2F, Pure Roppongi Bldg, 5-18-1 Roppongi, Minato-ku; ⏱ 5pm-late Mon-Sat; Ⓜ Hibiya & Toei Ōedo lines to Roppongi (exit 3)

More a German *izakaya* (pub-eatery) than a bar, the very friendly Bernd's is slightly removed from the mad parade of Roppongi Crossing. Hearty, authentic German food goes with the German draught *bier*. Menus are in German, Japanese and English – languages that the owner speaks with aplomb.

☥ GERONIMO
ジェロニモ *Bar*
☎ 3478 7449; www.geronimoshotbar .com; 2F, Yamamuro Bldg, 7-14-10 Roppongi, Minato-ku; ⏱ 6pm-6am Mon-Fri, 7pm-6am Sat & Sun; Ⓜ Hibiya & Toei Ōedo lines to Roppongi (exits 3 & 4)

Geronimo is poised over Roppongi Crossing, making it a logical place to start out a bar crawl through the neighbourhood. The place has a friendly vibe, and if you are feeling superfriendly you can bang on the drum that signals your intention to buy a round for everyone in the bar. *Kampai!*

☂ HEARTLAND
ハートランド *Bar*

☎ 5772 7600; 1F, West Walk, Roppongi Hills, 6-10-1 Roppongi, Minato-ku; ⏲ 5pm-4am; ⊖ Hibiya & Toei Ōedo lines to Roppongi (exits 1c & 3)

Okay, so you're a grownup and don't feel like starting your evening in a rowdy, sloppy shot bar, but you have to start somewhere, so head over to Heartland and introduce yourself to Heartland beer and the world of Roppongi-style, Japanese-*gaijin* relations.

☂ MADO LOUNGE
マドラウンジ *Lounge*

☎ 3470 0052; www.ma-do.jp; 52F, Mori Tower, 6-10-1 Roppongi Hills, Roppongi, Minato-ku; cover Sun-Thu ¥500, Fri & Sat ¥2000; ⏲ 10am-11.30pm Sun-Thu, 10am-3am Fri & Sat; ⊖ Hibiya & Toei Ōedo lines to Roppongi (exits 1c & 3)

On the 52nd floor of Mori Tower, the views are indeed stunning from this very cool window lounge. To get in, you'll have to first pay admission to the Mori Museum (p139) and/or Tokyo City View, so it's only worth the cover if you're here already.

☂ MADURO マデュロ *Lounge*

☎ 4333 8888; 4F, Grand Hyatt Tokyo, 6-10-3 Roppongi, Minato-ku; cover around ¥1500; ⏲ 6pm-2am Sun-Thu, 6pm-3am Fri & Sat; ⊖ Hibiya & Toei Ōedo lines to Roppongi (exits 1c & 3)

Make a dramatic entrance into Maduro from the 6th floor over the bridge and pond inside the labyrinthine Grand Hyatt Tokyo. Swanky and sleek, this is a chic spot to start your evening. There's live music nightly, but arrive before 9pm to avoid the cover.

★ PLAY

☆ ABBEY ROAD
アビーロード *Live music*

☎ 3402 0017; www.abbeyroad.ne.jp; B1F, Roppongi Annex Bldg, 4-11-5 Roppongi, Minato-ku; cover ¥1600-2100; ⏲ 6pm-midnight Mon-Thu, 6pm-1am Fri & Sat; ⊖ Hibiya & Toei Ōedo lines to Roppongi (exits 4a & 7)

Abbey Road is one of the two Roppongi clubs with uncannily good live Beatles tribute bands. Pull up a chair and prepare to be flabbergasted by the house Beatles cover bands – all Japanese, all seriousness, and appearances aside, pretty dang impressive. Aside from the cover, there's a two-drink minimum. Book ahead if you can, especially on weekends.

☆ BLUE NOTE ブルーノート
Live music

☎ 5485 0088; www.bluenote.co.jp; Raika Bldg, 6-3-16 Minami-Aoyama, Minato-ku; cover ¥6000-10,000; ⏲ 5.30pm-1am Mon-Sat, 5pm-12.30am Sun; ⊖ Chiyoda, Ginza, & Hanzōmon lines to Omote-sandō (exit B3)

Serious cognoscenti roll up at Tokyo's prime jazz spot, where you can get up close and personal with greats such as Maceo Parker and Chick Corea. From Roppongi-dōri, head up Kotto-dōri and hang a right at the 6th alley up.

☆ BUL-LET'S ブレッツ *Club*
☎ 3401 4844; www.bul-lets.com; B1F, Kasumi Bldg, 1-7-11 Nishi-Azabu, Minato-ku; cover from ¥1500; ⊕ Hibiya & Toei Ōedo lines to Roppongi (exits 2 & 3)
This mellow basement space plays worldwide trance and ambient sounds for barefoot patrons. Beds and sofas await for those who need a soft spot. But don't get the wrong idea – it's not all tranquillity and lazing away. Get your groove on to live electronica and experimental rhythms.

☆ CAVERN CLUB
キャヴァンクラブ
Live music
☎ 3405 5207; www.cavernclub.jp; 1F, Saito Bldg, 5-3-2 Roppongi, Minato-ku; cover women/men ¥1575/1890; ⊕ 6pm-2.30am; ⊕ Hibiya & Toei Ōedo lines to Roppongi (exit 3)
Eerily flawless renditions of Beatles covers have to be heard to be believed, sung by four Japanese mop-heads called the Silverbeats. This club is named for the place where the Beatles first appeared in Liverpool. Reserve a table ahead.

☆ CLUB 328 三二八 *Club*
☎ 3401 4968; www.3-2-8.jp; B1F, Kotsu Anzen Center Bldg, 3-24-20 Nishi-Azabu, Minato-ku; cover ¥2000-2500; ⊕ 8pm-5am; ⊕ Hibiya & Toei Ōedo lines to Roppongi (exits 1c & 3)
DJs at San-ni-pa (aka San-ni-hachi) spin a quality mix, from funk to reggae to R&B. With its refreshing un-Roppongi feel and a cool crowd of Japanese and *gaijin*, 328 is a good place to boogie 'til the break of dawn. Two drinks are included with the cover.

☆ EL CAFÉ LATINO
エルカフェラティーノ *Club*
☎ 3402 8989; www.elcafelatino.com; 2F, 3-15-24 Roppongi, Minato-ku; cover ¥1500-2000; ⊕ 6pm-midnight Tue-Thu & Sun, 6pm-5am Fri & Sat; ⊕ Hibiya & Toei Ōedo lines to Roppongi (exit 3)
Even if you don't know your merengue from your mambo, the dance teachers at Café Latino are pros at showing newbies how to bust the right moves. The energy and excellent mix of music draw consistent crowds here, one of the longest-running Latin dance clubs in the city.

☆ LOVENET ラブネット
Karaoke
☎ 5771 5511; www.lovenet-jp.com; 3F, Hotel Ibis, 7-14-4 Roppongi, Minato-ku; private ste ¥4000-60,000; ⊕ 6pm-5am; ⊕ Hibiya & Toei Ōedo lines to Roppongi (exit 4a)

Over-the-top, imaginatively themed private karaoke rooms range from more modest Arabian Suite to the Aqua Suite, whose drawcard is the Jacuzzi tub from which guests can warble their favourite hits. This is karaoke as only Roppongi can make it. Lovenet also has a full menu and bar to fuel your vocal exertions.

☆ MUSE ミューズ *Club*
☎ 5467 1188; www.muse-web.com; 4-1-1 Nishi-Azabu, Minato-ku; cover ¥3000; 🕐 7pm-late Sun-Mon, 9pm-late Tue-Thu & Sat, 8pm-late Fri; Ⓜ Hibiya & Toei Ōedo lines to Roppongi (exits 1b & 3)

With a friendly, international crowd, multilevel Muse has something for everyone – packed dance floor, several bar areas, cosy alcoves big enough for two, as well as pool tables, darts and karaoke. Women don't pay the weekend cover, which includes two drinks.

☆ NEW LEX-EDO ニューレックス エドゥ *Club*
☎ 3479 7477; www.newlex-edo.com; B1F, Gotō Bldg, 3-13-14 Roppongi, Minato-ku; cover women/men ¥3000/4000; 🕐 8pm-5am; Ⓜ Hibiya & Toei Ōedo lines to Roppongi (exit 3)

The Lex has forever been the club where visiting celebrities turn up, and though it's recently had a bit of a facelift, the scene retains its laid-back, fun atmosphere. Cover (waived if you've had your visage on the cover of *Vogue* or *Rolling Stone*) includes three free drinks.

☆ SALSA SUDADA サルサスダーダ *Club*
☎ 5474 8806; www.salsasudada.org; 3F, La Palette Bldg, 3F, 7-13-8 Roppongi, Minato-ku; cover ¥1500; 🕐 6pm-6am; Ⓜ Hibiya & Toei Ōedo lines to Roppongi (exits 3 & 4a)

Salsa and Latin dance have swept Tokyo off its feet, and Salsa Sudada is a popular haunt for local salsa and merengue dancers. Beginners can take lessons here early every evening, and then practise their new moves with the dancers from all over the world who frequent this place.

☆ STB 139 *Live Music*
☎ 5474 1395; http://stb139.co.jp; 6-7-11 Roppongi, Minato-ku; cover ¥3000-7000; 🕐 6-11pm Mon-Sat; Ⓜ Hibiya & Toei Ōedo lines to Roppongi (exit 3)

A two-minute walk south of Roppongi station, this is a large, lovely space that draws similarly big-name acts. Performances are predominantly jazz, covering the spectrum from acid to big band. Even if the act is unknown to you, the ambience will be wonderful and the standards high. Call for reservations between 11am and 8pm.

SHIATSU SESSIONS

Has Tokyo chewed you up and spat you out? Spring back to life with a shiatsu massage. One stop from Shinjuku station, Kimura-sensei at the **Kimura Shiatsu Institute** (off map p89; ☎ 3485 4515; www.shiatsu-k.com/english; Rm 713, 1-48-19 Sasazuka, Shibuya-ku; shiatsu from ¥5000; ◐ 10am-8pm; 🚇 Keiō line to Sasazuka station) not only practises but teaches shiatsu, and he speaks English. Or make an appointment with **Egbok Azabu Oriental Clinic** (☎ 3586 8909; Rm 301, Roppong Five Bldg, 5-18-20 Roppongi, Minato-ku; (shiatsu from ¥7300); ◐ 9.30am-10pm; 🚇 Hibiya or Toei Ōedo lines to Roppongi, exit 3). They offer Western-style massage, shiatsu and acupuncture, in studio or on house calls.

⭐ SUPERDELUXE スーパーデラックス *Live music*

☎ 5412 0515; www.super-deluxe.com; B1F, 3-1-25 Nishi-Azabu, Minato-ku; cover varies; ◐ 6pm-late Mon-Sat; 🚇 Hibiya & Toei Ōedo lines to Roppongi (exits 1b & 3)

Hard to categorise, easy to enjoy, SuperDeluxe morphs from lounge to gallery to club to performance space from night to night. Check the website for current events to see what's on, but you're guaranteed to run into a fabulous mix of creative types from Tokyo and beyond.

⭐ TOHO CINEMAS ROPPONGI HILLS 東宝シネマズ六本木ヒルズ *Cinema*

☎ 5775 6090; 6-10-2 Roppongi, Minato-ku; adult ¥1800-3000, concession ¥1000, 1st day of month ¥1000, women on Wed ¥1000; ◐ 10am-midnight Sun-Wed, 10am-5am Thu-Sat; 🚇 Hibiya & Toei Ōedo lines to Roppongi (exits 1c & 3)

Virgin's nine-screen multiplex has the biggest screen in Japan, as well as luxurious reclining seats and internet booking for reserved seats up to two days in advance. This state-of-the-art theatre also holds all-night screenings Thursday through Saturday, and on nights before holidays.

⭐ ULTRA LOUNGE *Club*

☎ 5775 3678; www.ultraloungetokyo .com; 3-9-5 Roppongi, Minato-ku; cover from ¥2000; ◐ 10pm-late Mon-Sat; 🚇 Hibiya & Toei Ōedo lines to Roppongi (exit 5)

Chill out with a bottle of Champagne and someone you want to wow at Ultra Lounge. The sound system is state-of-the-art, which is fine for lounge nights but fantastic on club nights, for which you'll want to show up dressed to order to make the cut.

>ODAIBA

Odaiba, an artificial island built on landfill in Tokyo Bay, is a great way to escape from Tokyo without leaving the city. Most people will arrive here via the driverless monorail from Shimbashi station, and will be treated with superb views of Tokyo and the bay. But this isn't all. Odaiba is an entertainment district, a setting for unconventional architecture and a showcase for futuristic innovations, displayed in museums and show-rooms around town. Kids couldn't get bored here, between the Tokyo Joypolis (an indoor, high-tech amusement park), the world's biggest Ferris wheel and excellent museums whose exhibits include remote-controlled boats. Lovers of kitsch will be equally delighted to come across the replica of the Statue of Liberty and the theme parks made in the images of old Edo, Hong Kong and even 17th-century Italy (a bathhouse, restaurant row and shopping mall, respectively). If there's a comprehensive theme to the architecture of Odaiba, you could call it 'experimental', but mostly it stands as a record of the 'bubble era' and the futuristic aesthetics and intentions of that period.

ODAIBA

👁 SEE

Because Odaiba doesn't have the typical glut of traffic that mainland Tokyo has, the island is quite pleasant to traverse on foot. But if you're covering a lot of ground between museums and malls and *onsen* (hot springs), you might opt to take the free shuttle bus that makes a circuit around Odaiba between 11am and 8pm. The red buses come around every 15 minutes or so and stop at a dozen locations on the island, including Aqua City and Fuji TV. Bus stops are not signposted in English but have red markers with bus symbols on them.

👁 FUJI TV フジテレビ

☎ 5500 8888; 2-4-8 Daiba, Minato-ku; observation deck ¥500/300; 🕙 10am-8pm Tue-Sun; 🚉 Rinkai line to Tokyo Teleport or Yurikamome line to Odaiba Kaihin-kōen

Designed by the late, great Kenzō Tange, the Fuji TV headquarters building is recognisable by the 90-degree angles of its scaffold-inglike structure, topped with a 1200-tonne ball. You can actually go into the ball, which is a terrific observation deck. Pick up an English guide at the information desk out front, and take a self-guided tour.

👁 MUSEUM OF MARITIME SCIENCE 船の科学館

☎ 5500 1111; www.funenokagakukan .or.jp; 3-1 Higashi-Yashio, Shinagawa-ku; admission ¥700/400; 🕙 10am-5pm Tue-Sun; 🚉 Yurikamome line to Fune-no-Kagakukan; ♿ 🚼

This is one of Tokyo's better museums, containing four floors of excellent displays with loads of detailed models, lots of hands-on exhibits that kids will love, and a pool on the roof where, for ¥100, they can wreak havoc with radio-controlled boats and submarines.

👁 NATIONAL MUSEUM OF EMERGING SCIENCE & INNOVATION (MIRAIKAN) 日本科学未来館

☎ 3570 9151; www.miraikan.jst.go.jp; 2-41 Aomi, Kōtō-ku; admission ¥500/200, kids free on Sat; 🕙 10am-5pm Wed-Mon; 🚉 Yurikamome line to Fune-no-Kagakukan or Telecom Center; ♿ 🚼

Kids will love the engaging exhibits at this science museum, where most displays have excellent explanations in English and English-speaking guides fill in the blanks. There's the spectacular planetarium (buy tickets for a show as soon as you arrive), demonstrations of robots and opportunities to interact with them, and tons of exhibits about space, medicine and the environment.

◎ TOKYO BIG SIGHT
東京ビッグサイト

☎ 5530 1111; www.bigsight.jp/english;
3-21-1 Ariake, Kōtō-ku; ◉ Rinkai line
to Kokusai-Tenjijō or Yurikamome line
to Kokusai-Tenjijō-Seimon; ♿

Odaiba is full of oddball
architecture and Tokyo Big
Sight (officially known as Tokyo
International Exhibition Hall) is
certainly no exception – appro-
priate, since it is the semi-annual
venue for Tokyo's coolest design
festival, Design Festa (p107).
Keep a look out for the upside-
down pyramids of the conference
tower rising above the exhibition
complex.

🛍 SHOP

🛍 DECKS TOKYO BEACH
デックス東京ビーチ
Department store

☎ 3599 6500; www.odaiba-decks.com;
1-6-1 Daiba, Minato-ku; ⏰ 11am-9pm;
🚉 Yurikamome line to Odaiba
Kaihin-kōen; ♿ &

Fashioned after a beachside
boardwalk, Decks Tokyo Beach is
split into two sides: the Seaside
Mall and Island Mall. Both house
shopping and dining, and this
is also the place you'll find the
indoor amusement park, Tokyo
Joypolis (p159).

◎ VENUS FORT
ヴィーナスフォート
Department store

☎ 3599 0700; www.venusfort.co.jp;
Palette Town, Aomi 1-chōme, Kōtō-ku;
⏰ 11am-9pm, restaurants 11am-11pm;
🚉 Yurikamome line to Aomi or Rinkai
line to Tokyo Teleport; ♿

Venus Fort embodies a Japanese vision of a young woman's
shopping paradise, in a building
that mimics 17th-century Rome
where the ceilings simulate the
sky turning from day to night.
With around 170 boutiques and
restaurants all aimed at young
women, this kitschy shopping
centre also boasts the distinction
of having Japan's biggest lavatory
(64 stalls).

Open skies inside the Romanesque Venus Fort

🍴 EAT

🍴 DAIBA LITTLE HONG KONG

Food-themed park   ¥¥

☎ 3599 6500; 6F & 7F, Decks Tokyo Beach, 1-6-1 Daiba, Minato-ku; ⏱ 11am-10pm; 🚉 Yurikamome line to Ōdaiba Kaihin-Kōen; ♿ 🚻

Among the quirky attractions of Odaiba is this kooky replica of Hong Kong's streets, complete with a recorded soundtrack of simulated street noise, neon signs, souvenir shops and restaurants slinging *gyōza* (dumplings) and *yum cha*.

🍴 KHAZANA カザーナ

Indian   ¥

☎ 3599 6551; 5F, Decks Tokyo Beach, 1-6-1 Daiba, Minato-ku; ⏱ 11am-11pm; 🚉 Yurikamome line to Ōdaiba Kaihin-Kōen; ♿ Ⓥ 🚻

Come early to snag one of the coveted tables out on the deck for maximum sensory pleasure. This Indian restaurant serves a good all-you-can-eat buffet lunch and has a fair number of vegetarian options on the menu.

🍴 TSUKIJI TAMA SUSHI 築地玉寿司

Sushi & sashimi   ¥¥

☎ 3599 6556; 5F, Decks Tokyo Beach, 1-6-1 Daiba, Minato-ku; ⏱ 11am-11pm; 🚉 Yurikamome line to Odaiba Kaihin-kōen

Seat yourself near the windows and sip from a huge cup of green tea while you wait for your sushi – it will come immaculately presented and perfectly fresh. The menu also includes set meals and *udon*.

🍸 DRINK

HANASHIBE はなしべ

Izakaya

☎ 3599 5575; 3F, Aqua City, 1-7-1 Daiba, Minato-ku; ⏱ 11am-11pm; 🚉 Yurikamome line to Daiba; ♿ 🚻

For Kyoto specialities and house-brewed sake, check out Hanashibe in the Mediage entertainment complex in Aqua City. You can try three types of sake in a tasting set (¥700), which you can match with small dishes typical of an *izakaya* (pub eatery).

🍸 SUNSET BEACH BREWING COMPANY サンセットビーチブルーイングカンパニー

Brewery

☎ 3599 6655; 5F, Decks Tokyo Beach, 1-6-1 Daiba, Minato-ku; ⏱ 11am-11pm; 🚉 Yurikamome line to Ōdaiba Kaihin-Kōen; 🚻

After roaming around Odaiba put your feet up and enjoy expansive views with an island-brewed beer. There are reasonably priced lunch and dinner buffets, but the house Italian food isn't worth the trip.

⭐ PLAY

CINEMA MEDIAGE
シネマメディアージュ
Cinema

☎ 5531 7878; 1F & 2F, Mediage, Aqua City, 1-7-1 Daiba, Minato-ku; tickets ¥1800/1500/1000, women ¥1000 on Wed; 🕓 ticket sales 11am-11pm; 🚉 Yurikamome line to Daiba; ♿
This enormous 3000-seat multiplex shows Japanese and foreign films, many of which are subtitled and some of which are dubbed into Japanese. Check the *Japan Times* or *Metropolis* for current listings. Mediage is located inside the Aqua City shopping centre.

⭐ MUSCLE PARK マッスル
パーク *Amusement Park*

☎ 6821 0091; www.musclepark.jp; 5F, Island Mall, Decks Tokyo Beach, 1-6-1 Daiba, Minato-ku; admission ¥1000-3900/600-1000; 🕓 11am-9pm Sun-Fri, 11am-10pm Sat; 🚉 Yurikamome line to Ōdaiba Kaihin-Kōen; 👶
A rarity in Tokyo, where much of the high-tech entertainment is of the sedentary variety, this amusement space features physical challenges and games from popular TV shows and even includes a kids park.

⭐ ŌEDO ONSEN MONOGATARI
天江戸温泉物語 *Hot spring*

☎ 5500 1126; www.ooedoonsen.jp /english; 2-57 Aomi, Kōtō-ku; admission ¥2900/1600; 🕓 11am-9am, last entry at 7am; 🚉 Yurikamome line to Telecom Center
This *onsen* is set up like an Edo-era town and pipes in natural mineral water from 1400m beneath Tokyo Bay. Although the setup might seem cheesy, the *onsen* is attractively designed, with old-fashioned restaurants and souvenir shops for a postbath bite and browse. Admission fees cover the rental of *yukata* (cotton kimonos) and towels. Fees vary between morning and night, so check the website for full details.

⭐ TOKYO JOYPOLIS
東京ジョイポリス
Amusement park

☎ 5500 1801; 3F-5F, Decks Tokyo Beach, 1-6-1 Daiba, Minato-ku; passport ¥3500/3100, after 5pm ¥2500/2100; 🕓 10am-11pm; 🚉 Yurikamome line to Odaiba Kaihin-Kōen; ♿ 👶
Joypolis is Sega's high-tech playland for overstimulating your kids, or yourself. Your visit here will be full of nonstop action, with crazy indoor roller coasters, video games and virtual-reality rides.

Tokyoites rise early and work late; they're always on the move and connected to their *ketai* (mobile phones). Since most live in cramped quarters, entertaining and socialising happens outside the home. Subsequently, Tokyo's mix of social and cultural activities, galleries and eateries provide the perfect backdrop for a varied and rich experience.

A kaleidoscope of colours bloom in the Imperial Palace East Garden (p48)

ACCOMMODATION

Staying anywhere along the Yamanote loop (p194) gives you easy access to nearly every corner of the city. If it's not on the loop, some subway line will quickly connect you. Central Tokyo hotels put you in strolling distance of Ginza shopping and myriad dining options, while Shinjuku has a slew of solid hotels catering to business travellers. Ebisu doesn't have many places to stay, but is a quieter, stylish part of the city that's also connected to the Yamanote loop. For those who want nothing to do with quiet nights in, staying around Roppongi means being able to stumble to bed at any hour without worrying about the trains shutting down at midnight. Additionally, despite its reputation as an exorbitantly expensive city to visit, Tokyo does have pleasant budget options, including capsule hotels, generic but reasonably-priced 'business hotels' and some excellent ryokan (Japanese-style inns).

Ryokan in Tokyo don't fit the traditional definition in the strictest sense – in this city, they typically won't include meals, and on the budget end you may even have to bring (or buy) your own towel. Most have tatami (woven floor matting) floors; you should always remove your shoes or slippers before entering a tatami room. At a typical Japanese ryokan, a futon is usually laid out and made up in the evenings, then folded up and put away in the mornings; however, in budget ryokan you'll do this yourself or simply leave the futon out all day. Be sure to also take advantage of at least one soak in the *sentō* (public baths; see p176) available here, an experience most modern hotels don't offer. You'll find most of Tokyo's ryokan in Asakusa and Ueno.

Need a place to stay? Find and book it at lonelyplanet.com. Over 120 properties are featured for Tokyo – each personally visited, thoroughly reviewed and happily recommended by a Lonely Planet author. From hostels to high-end hotels, we've hunted out the places that will bring you unique and special experiences. Read independent reviews by authors and other travellers, and get practical information including amenities, maps and photos. Then reserve your room simply and securely via Hotels & Hostels – our online booking service. It's all at lonelyplanet.com/hotels.

Seekers of Japanese kitsch will want to stay in one of the famed love hotels (p121). These days they're more politely referred to as 'boutique' or 'fashion' hotels, and there's one for every taste, from miniature Gothic castles to Middle-Eastern temples – and these are just the buildings. Some rooms even have bath grottoes or ceiling swings. Love hotels are most highly concentrated on Love Hotel Hill (p120).

Solo travellers could also check into that uniquely Japanese invention: the capsule hotel. Making the most of limited space, these individual capsules are not as cheap as you might imagine (around ¥4000), but they are tall enough for lounging and come outfitted with personal TVs. Personal storage space is limited to lockers, so don't bring a ton of baggage; personal space is obviously at a premium, so do bring earplugs.

To search for and book Tokyo accommodations, check out www.jpinn.com for ryokan, and www.japanhotelfinder.com or Lonely Planet's own online booking service (see the boxed text opposite).

BEST RYOKAN

> Ginza Yoshimizu (www.yoshimizu.com/en/ginza/index.html)
> Kimi Ryokan (www.kimi-ryokan.jp)
> Ryokan Shigetsu (www.shigetsu.com)
> Sawanoya Ryokan (www.sawanoya.com)
> Sukeroku no Yado Sadachiyo (www.sadachiyo.co.jp)

BEST LUXURY HOTELS

> Four Seasons Chinzan-sō (www.fourseasons.com/tokyo)
> Ritz-Carlton Tokyo (www.ritzcarlton.com/en/properties/tokyo)
> Grand Hyatt (www.grandhyatttokyo.com)
> Four Seasons Marunouchi (www.fourseasons.com/marunouchi)
> Park Hyatt (http://tokyo.park.hyatt.com)

BEST BUSINESS BETS

> Hotel Century Southern Tower (www.southerntower.co.jp)
> Mercure Ginza (www.mercure.com/gb/hotel-5701-mercure-hotel-ginza-tokyo/index.shtml)
> Mitsui Garden Hotel (www.gardenhotels.co.jp/eng/ginza)
> Park Hotel Tokyo (www.parkhoteltokyo.com)
> Cerulean Tower Tōkyū Hotel (www.ceruleantower-hotel.com/en)
> Westin Hotel Tokyo (www.westin-tokyo.co.jp)

BEST BOUTIQUE HOTELS

> Granbell Hotel (www.granbellhotel.jp)
> Hotel Claska (www.claska.com)
> Hotel Seiyō Ginza (www.seiyo-ginza.com)

SNAPSHOTS

ANIME & MANGA

Akihabara is *the* manga Mecca for Tokyoites and visitors alike, and is even becoming an attraction for those seeking a glimpse of the distinctly Japanese *otaku* (geek) subculture. It's the best place to start a quest for manga. The burly Mandarake chain, whose exhaustive flagship is located in Nakano, has a large outpost here, filled with all manner of manga from the kid-friendly *Doraemon* (a blue robotic cat from the future) to *dōjinshi* (self-published, fan-drawn spin-offs and parodies) to *hentai* (perverse) manga, DVDs, games and figurines.

One of the richest treasure-troves in the city is the chain bookshop Book Off, which buys and sells used manga and has an entire section of paperbacks for only ¥100 apiece. You could easily collect an entire series for what amounts to lunch money. There's also a burgeoning female *otaku* culture (see the boxed text, p85) and its own geek haven in Ikebukuro, a hotbed of the 'boys' love' manga genre.

BEST PLACES TO PERUSE
> Mandarake (p122)
> Tora no Ana (p57)

BEST MUSEUMS TO VISIT
> Ghibli Museum (p91)
> Yayoi & Yumeji Takehisa Museums (p71)

BEST OTAKU HANGOUTS
> Akihabara (p44)
> Otome Rd (p85)

ARCHITECTURE

After WWII incendiary bombing flattened much of Tokyo, the city collected itself and began the long decades of reconstruction. Tokyo hit a boom period in the '50s, during which the subway system started to take shape. And when the city won the privilege of hosting the 1964 summer Olympics, buildings seemed to sprout like mushrooms after a long rain. One of the structures built for the Olympics was the National Yoyogi Stadium, a structure of curves sloping down from a suspension roof. The building was designed by Kenzō Tange, an Osaka-born architect who taught at Tokyo University and died in 2005. During his long career he influenced the reshaping of the cityscape, and his designs stand out all over Tokyo.

But diversity reigns in the vibrant architectural face of the city. Although not the most sustainable strategy, aging buildings are demolished to make way for bigger, newer and ever more innovative structures that astound and inspire. Because real estate is at a premium in this denser-than-dense megalopolis, the only way to go is up.

BEST STRUCTURAL STATEMENTS
> National Diet Building (p142)
> Roppongi Hills (p138)
> Tokyo International Forum (p51)
> Tokyo Metropolitan Government Offices (p91)

BEST COPYCATS
> Statue of Liberty (p154; pictured right)
> Tokyo Tower (p143)

MOST FASHIONABLE & FUNCTIONAL
> BAPExclusive (p108)
> Comme des Garcons (p108)
> Hanae Mori Building (p109)
> Prada Aoyama (p106)

FOOD

Epicureans will find no shortage of new tastes to sample in the city, where renowned chefs from around the world set up shop, balancing out Tokyo's wasabi and soy sauce with balsamic vinegar and olive oil. A taste of the traditional can be sampled in venues as humble as the local *rāmen* shop or in the refined, minimalist tatami room of a *kaiseki* (elegant, multicourse Japanese meals) restaurant, while there's also an incredible diversity of international cuisine, representing culinary traditions from Sweden to Senegal. And of course comfort foods like burgers or pasta – though usually Japanese renditions of those dishes – are easily found across the city.

Japanese food runs the gamut between the raw fish of your sushi or sashimi platter and the deep-fried *panko* (Japanese breadcrumb) crust of a crispy, tender pork cutlet *(tonkatsu)* on a bed of shredded cabbage. In addition to *tonkatsu*, there's tempura and *kushi-katsu* (deep-fried skewers of meat and vegetables), both of which are often served in small courses, as they are cooked so that everything comes to the table piping hot. If on an oppressively humid day the last thing you want to eat is fried food, do as the Tokyoites do and have an *unagi* (barbecued eel) lunch to keep up your stamina. *Unagi* is especially tasty when it's grilled perfectly in its sweet soy marinade and served in a *bentō* (boxed meal) over rice. An even cooler (temperature-wise) option is cold *soba* (buckwheat noodles) that you dip in cold broth and slurp noisily. *Soba* can also be served hot, as are *udon* (thick wheat noodles) and *rāmen*.

Cook-it-yourself affairs such as sukiyaki or *shabu-shabu* are the most fun with a few people, where the morsels of simmered meat and vegetables are meant to be shared and the communal pot is tended by all. You can do the DIY experience alone, cooking up *okonomiyaki* or *monjayaki* – egg-batter pancakes full of cabbage, vegetables, seafood and meat – at your own table.

Adventurous eaters can also have a festive meal of *fugu* (puffer fish), that famously poisonous *poisson* that is safely prepared by trained experts. *Fugu* restaurants usually offer multicourse dinners featuring *fugu* sashimi, *shabu-shabu*, and *fugu* cooked a dozen ways. While the taste and texture of *fugu* may not wow you like the transcendent tuna of your sushi lunch, eating tuna doesn't come with the same satisfaction of having cheated death at the dinner table.

In general, most restaurants, whatever the type, often serve tasty *teishoku* (lunch sets) that are more reasonably priced than their dinner courses; keep this in mind if you wish to dine somewhere at the higher end of the spectrum, as lunch will often fit into your budget even if supper won't. Lunch sets at department store *resutoran-gai* ('restaurant towns') are very economical and tend to be of good quality. Browse the plastic food models and choose the shops specialising in one thing: *unagi*, tempura, *kushi-katsu*, sushi or *soba*. And if you just need something to tide you over for the next museum stop, convenience-store *onigiri* (rice ball; around ¥125) and iced tea is always just around the corner.

BEST UPMARKET JAPANESE
> Inakaya (p146)
> Kikunoi (p147)
> Kyūbei (p60)
> Ten-Ichi (p61)
> Ume-no-Hana (p116)

BEST FUSION
> Daidaiya (p96)
> Den Rokuen-tei (p124)
> Fujimamas (p112)
> Vin Chou (p80)

BEST BITES ON A BUDGET
> Hiroba (p113)
> Ippūdō (p134)
> Kantipur (p125)
> Sometarō (p80)

BEST SHITAMACHI ATMOSPHERE
> Hantei (p72)
> Kanda Yabu Soba (p60)
> Komagata Dojō (p79)

Opposite Feast your eyes on a delicate arrangement of sushi

GALLERIES

You can't really turn anywhere in Tokyo without seeing evidence of its thriving, dynamic visual arts scene. No self-respecting commercial district in Tokyo goes without its major department stores, and no department store worth its grand façade would dream of not installing an art gallery on one of its upper floors. Ginza is good place to start a gallery-hop. Between its department store *grandes dames* and its well-established art galleries, there's a hefty concentration of classy exhibition spaces. For more experimental fare, you might also venture into Ura-Hara (p102), the back alleys off of Omote-sandō, and then still further west into Aoyama.

Japanese art has historically blurred the lines between art and craft, high and low, and this is reflected in many of the works you'll find in Tokyo's galleries. Graphic-style art is ubiquitous, but installation, sculpture, electronic media, painting and photography are well represented – sometimes all in one bright package.

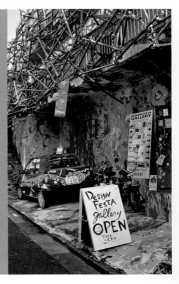

BEST MIXED BAG
> Design Festa Gallery (p107; pictured)
> Japan Traditional Crafts Center (p85)
> Watari Museum of Contemporary Art (p107)

BEST NEIGHBOURHOODS FOR GALLERY CRAWLS
> Aoyama (p103)
> Ginza (p52)
> Marunouchi (p45)

TOP GINZA STALWARTS
> Ginza Graphic Gallery (p45)
> Leica Ginza Salon (p50)
> Shiseido Gallery (p50)

BEST DEPARTMENT-STORE GALLERIES
> Laforet Museum (p103)
> Parco Factory (p120)

GAY & LESBIAN

Tokyo is more tolerant than most of its Asian counterparts in regards to homosexuality and alternative lifestyles, as long as public displays of affection are kept on the down-low. The active international scene encompasses a healthy club and bar life, newsletters and support groups. Intriguing cultural phenomena include the relatively mainstream theatre of the all-women Tokyo Takarazuka Gekijō (p65), which attracts all manner of housewives and young women with crushes on the drag-king actors. Meanwhile, the defining feature of *otome* (p85) – the female version of *otaku* (p123) – is a shared obsession with 'boys' love' manga that depicts the romantic relationships between gay males. While on the ground level, Tokyo society does not actively acknowledge the non-heterosexual population, its existence is normalised in a rich array of art forms and as a fact of fantasy life dissociated from quotidian concerns. So while the societal sanctions may be don't-ask, don't-tell, the social scene is alive and kicking.

For more information on the GLBT scene in Tokyo, check out the city guides on www.fridae.com and www.utopia-asia.com. Also look for the current issue of *Tokyo Journal* (p196), online and in print, for local listings on gay events and venues.

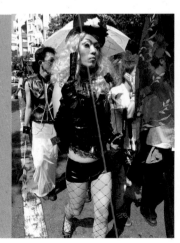

BEST BARS
> Advocates Bar (p97)
> Arch (p98)
> Arty Farty (p98)
> Kinswomyn (p99)

TOP EVENTS
> Tokyo Pride Parade (p33; pictured right)
> Tokyo International Lesbian & Gay Film Festival (p32)

V

KIDS

Tokyo is a child-friendly, attention-deficit paradise, and foreign kids will find distractions aplenty in the cute toys, electronic gadgetry, weird candy, high-tech toilets and noisy *pachinko* games. All those novel things you'll pass on the streets will catch their interest, like *fugu* (poisonous puffer fish) jetting around the tanks in front of restaurants, or the flashing neon in Shinjuku and Shibuya. On weekends the parks are full of weird and wonderful culture that both adults and kids will get a kick out of – the rockabilly dancers of Yoyogi Park (p28) and the *cosplay-zoku* of Jingū-bashi (p12), for starters. But for specifically child-centric entertainments, Tokyo has many pleasure districts. Amusement parks, fun museums and tantalising toy stores abound in this, the world capital of *kawaii* (cute). The Ghibli Museum (p91) is a must, but be absolutely sure to book your appointment well in advance.

Restaurants often provide childrens menus or special set meals, and even picky eaters who might turn their noses up at sashimi will love tender, crunchy *tonkatsu* (deep-fried pork cutlets) or *yakitori* (grilled chicken on a stick) and noodles. And if you're desperate, convenience stores and fast-food chains exist everywhere for the little ones who subsist solely on burgers and pizza.

BEST PLACES TO WIND 'EM UP & RUN 'EM DOWN
> Muscle Park (p159)
> Namco Namjatown (p86)
> Paddle boating (p92)
> Tokyo Disneyland (p52)
> Tokyo Joypolis (p159)
> Tokyo Metropolitan Children's Hall (p129)

BEST SPOTS FOR YOUR KIDS TO EMPTY YOUR POCKETS
> Hakuhinkan Toy Park (p54)
> Kiddyland (p110)
> Loft (p122)
> Tōkyū Hands (p94)

BEST KID-FRIENDLY INTERACTIVE MUSEUMS
> Museum of Maritime Science (p156)
> National Museum of Emerging Science & Innovation (p156)
> National Science Museum (p68)
> Shitamachi History Museum (p68)
> Taikokan (p77)

BEST PLACES TO OGLE ANIMALS (LIVING & DEAD)
> Meguro Parasitological Museum (p132)
> Sunshine International Aquarium (p84)
> Tsukiji Market (p51)
> Ueno Zoo (p71)

LIVE MUSIC

Aficionados of all genres will find kindred souls in Tokyo, whether your aural medication of choice is jazz, electronica, Motown, punk, classical, *reggaetón* or hip-hop. Big international acts like U2 regularly play Tokyo, as do popular home-grown musicians such as J-pop songstress Hikaru Utada and jazz instrumentalists P'ez. Smaller venues often book more underground bands, which you might not see in such intimate environs abroad. Check *Metropolis* (www.metropolis.co.jp) or *Tokyo Journal* (http://tokyo.to) for current listings.

While 'live houses' are scattered all over the city, the best are naturally centred in active, hip neighbourhoods such as Shibuya, Ebisu and Roppongi. Live shows tend to keep school-night hours so that music fans can hop their trains before midnight, and it's best to purchase tickets beforehand from the venue itself, or using **Ticket Pia** (☎ 0570-029 999; http://t.pia.co.jp in Japanese) with the help of a Japanese-speaking friend.

BEST LIVE HOUSES
> Club Quattro (p127)
> Crocodile (p116)
> La.mama (p128)
> Liquid Room (p136)
> Loft (p100)
> Shibuya O-West (p129)

BEST JAZZ JOINTS
> Blue Note (p150)
> JZ Brat (p128)
> Shinjuku Pit Inn (p101)
> STB 139 (p152)

BEST BEATLES ACTS
> Abbey Road (p150)
> Cavern Club (p151)

SNAPSHOTS

MARKETS

Street markets are not such a large part of Tokyo's urban landscape as they are in other cities, as stratospheric real estate costs make open spaces prohibitively expensive. That said, one of Tokyo's highlights happens to be one of the few markets in town. Tsukiji Market, which moves more than 2000 tonnes of seafood every day, is slated to move to new digs sometime around 2012, so catch it here while you can. Blueprints for the new market plan for a larger, more modern space that visitors won't be able to get into as down and dirty as they can now.

The open spaces of some temple grounds become commercial squares on various Sundays. While it's unlikely that you'll find truly rare antiques at these flea markets, there's usually some decent vintage kimonos, metalwork, lacquerware and interesting odds and ends to browse. Most markets close down by around 3pm. Also operating outdoors is the unusual Ameyoko Arcade in Ueno, where you can wander among the stalls of dried squid and discount sneakers. And of course, Tokyo's take on the traditional market is the bountiful, beautiful *depachika*.

BEST TEMPLE FLEA MARKETS
> Hanazono-jinja (open all Sun except in May & Nov; p90)
> Tōgō-jinja (open 1st, 4th & 5th Sun; p106)

BEST MARKET HIGHLIGHTS
> Ameyoko Arcade (p71)
> Tsukiji Market (p13)

MUSEUMS

The cup runneth over for museum-lovers in this city. Not only are there art museums displaying archaeological artefacts from a couple of thousand years ago and contemporary works in all manner of media, but tiny one-room shacks showcasing only buttons or *byōbu* (folding screens). Some of Tokyo's top museums have only been around for a few years, like the wonderfully multifaceted experience of the Edo-Tokyo Museum (p65) and the sky-high singularity of the Mori Art Museum (p139) at Roppongi Hills.

If you'll be in town for an extended period of time or expect to hit several museums during your visit, consider picking up a Grutt Pass (p71) to save a significant amount on what can add up to be hefty admission fees.

BEST TOKYO MUSEUMS

> Edo-Tokyo Museum (p65)
> National Museum of Modern Art (p50)
> Ōta Memorial Art Museum (p103)
> Tokyo Metropolitan Museum of Photography (p132)
> Tokyo National Museum (p69)

QUIRKIEST SHOWCASES

> Beer Museum Yebisu (p132)
> Criminology Museum of Meiji University (p45)

> Kite Museum (p49)
> Meguro Parasitological Museum (p132)
> Tobacco & Salt Museum (p121)

BEST FOR CONTEMPORARY ART

> Hara Museum of Contemporary Art (p120)
> Mori Art Museum (p139)
> National Art Center Tokyo (p139)
> Watarium (p107)

V

SNAPSHOTS

NIGHTLIFE

Tokyo's thriving nightlife means no shortage of bars, karaoke lounges, dance clubs and *izakaya* (pub-eatery) populating every corner of the city. But for choice, some neighbourhoods are better than others. Roppongi has historically been the centre of rowdy all-night ragers, where military goons and newly arrived expats collide with hard-partying locals looking for foreign action. But it's not all downscale pick-up joints, and the diversity of clubs and bars all located in one area make it the obvious destination for a night out. Still, it's not the last word in nightlife – Love Hotel Hill on Shibuya's Dōgenzaka is packed with clubs, large live-music venues, and bars and *izakaya*. These clubs attract those in their 20s, and the music tends to be mainstream (ie hip-hop, marquee Japanese pop and flavour-of-the-month). For the slightly older and more indie-inclined, there are the hip clubs and bars of Ebisu and Daikanyama. East Shinjuku is probably the least pretentious of these hotspots.

Clubs typically charge a cover from ¥1500 to ¥3000, usually including a drink or two. Weekend covers tend to be higher than on weeknights, and at some venues men and women are charged differently. Some clubs give discounts if you bring in a flyer (check their websites, or the record stores around Shibuya), and it's often a good idea to bring a photo ID.

BEST TOP-VIEW BARS
> Asahi Sky Room (p80)
> Mado Lounge (p150)
> New York Bar (p99)

BEST UNPRETENTIOUS CLUBS
> Club 328 (p151)
> Muse (p152)
> New Lex-Edo (p152)
> Unit (p137)
> Salsa Sudada (p152)

BEST BARS FOR LOOKING & LOUNGING
> Aux Amis des Vins (p62)
> Den Aquaroom (p116)
> Insomnia Lounge (p126)
> Maduro (p150)

BEST SAKE IZAKAYA
> Sakana-tei (p125)
> Sasashū (p87)
> Takara (p62)

PARKS & GARDENS

Apartment-dwellers of Tokyo may not have the luxury of gardens, but they have hectares of open space in the city's large parks. All parks in Tokyo are free with the notable exception of Shinjuku-gyoen, and they provide respite and refuge from the rhythms of urban life. On weekdays you're likely to get a laid-back experience at the city's parks and gardens, but weekends see them at their best, when families and couples turn out for strolls and picnics.

During *hanami* (cherry-blossom viewing; p31) season, blue tarps are spread on the grass and the sake flows at *hanami* parties crowding popular parks such as Shinjuku-gyoen and Ueno-kōen. From around mid-October to early November, *kōyō* (autumn foliage season) brings its spectacular palette of golds, yellows, oranges and fiery scarlet hues to parks including Yoyogi-kōen and Koishikawa-Kōrakuen (p49).

The beautifully landscaped gardens of Tokyo make even better escapes. Gardens usually charge a small admission fee, and on weekdays you're likely to have the carp ponds and well-groomed paths practically to yourself.

BEST PARKS
> Shinjuku-gyoen (p91)
> Ueno-kōen (p66)
> Yoyogi-kōen (p107)

MOST GORGEOUS GARDENS
> Dembō-in (p76)
> Hama-rikyū-teien (p48)
> Imperial Palace East Garden (p48; pictured right)
> Meiji-jingū-gyoen (p103)
> National Institute for Nature Study (p132)

BEST PLACES FOR HANAMI
> Hama-rikyū-teien (p48)
> Shinjuku-gyoen (p91)
> Ueno-kōen (p66)

SENTŌ & ONSEN

As much for gossip as for hygiene, *sentō* (public baths) and *onsen* (hot springs) are pulse points for strengthening social bonds in Japan. Although modern dwellings have bath facilities, many Tokyoites bathe regularly at *sentō* and often go with friends or family members. The metropolitan government generously subsidises the city's *sentō* and *onsen*, making them inexpensive (admission around ¥500) and easily accessible to everyone.

In Tokyo, where both institutions do business in modern buildings, the difference between *sentō* and *onsen* may not seem clear. The essential distinction is that *sentō* can heat up their own tap water, but water at an *onsen* must come from a natural hot spring. The concept of a such a bubbling spring existing in this paved-over urban wilderness might sound laughable, but natural sources underneath Tokyo Bay actually do supply the city's *onsen* with mineral-rich, dark water.

Bathing communally in traditional Japanese baths is an excellent balm for the stresses of the streets and a transcendent experience even if the backdrop isn't the rushing waterfall of a mountain resort. In them you'll encounter people of all ages and walks of life, and catch a glimpse of city folk at their most relaxed. For more information see p101.

BEST KITSCHY ONSEN EXPERIENCE
> Ōedo Onsen Monogatari (p159; pictured right)

BEST OLD-SCHOOL NEIGHBOURHOOD ONSEN
> Jakotsu-yu Onsen (p81)
> Asakusa Kannon Onsen (p81)

SHRINES & TEMPLES

Japan's two major religions, Shintōism and Buddhism, have coexisted peacefully and influenced each other for more than a thousand years. Shintō's animistic tradition, which views the environment as one inhabited with *kami* (gods or spirits), is Japan's native religion. Buddhism, and its belief in the cycle of reincarnation, was an import from India by way of China and Korea.

In day-to-day life most Tokyoites do not consider themselves religious, conducting and participating in religious ceremonies only at those defining moments of birth, marriage and death. But while Shintōism may not play an overt role in people's lives, its basic tenets have seeped so deeply into the Japanese culture that they are inseparable from what are considered quotidian matters. For example, the Shintō practice of purification isn't limited to the rinsing of mouths and hands at the entrance of shrines, but also led to the lasting tradition of the thorough, ritualistic cleansing at *sentō*.

Shintō shrines honour *kami*, which also reside in natural features such as waterfalls and mountains. Once a person dies, they too become a *kami*, but upon death Buddhism defines the funereal rituals. Keep this in mind when you notice that Buddhist temples often house cemeteries, while Shintō shrines do not. Shintō shrines range in size from tiny *inari* (fox deity) shrines occupying narrow spaces between buildings to the grand Meiji-jingū (p103), and are scattered far and wide across Tokyo. Long-established Buddhist temples also dot the cityscape in every neighbourhood and make up an integral part of the community.

BEST SHRINES
> Asakusa-jinja (p76)
> Chingodō-ji (p76)
> Hie-jinja (p139)
> Tōshōgū (p69)
> Yasukuni-jinja (p51)

BEST TEMPLES
> Benten-dō (p68)
> Kiyomizu Kannon-dō (p68)
> Meiji-jingū (p103; pictured right)
> Sensō-ji (p77)

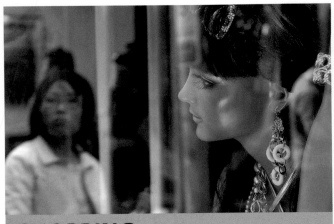

SHOPPING

Shopping is a serious endeavour in this city: it's the number-one recreational activity. It's therapy, investment, and a way to socialise and show off status. It's also intertwined with ritual and expectation – on Valentine's Day, women are expected to give *giri* (obligation) chocolate to all the men in their lives, and it ain't for love. Shopping is part of the Tokyo lifestyle, and gift-giving is a tradition that has evolved into an art. It's no wonder, then, that this city is a candy store for the consumer with cash. And you don't need a lot of it for inexpensive treats like delicate *washi* (handmade paper), kitchen tools and stationery at ¥100 shops and small Japanese toys.

Stores are generally open daily but closed on one Monday or Wednesday of each month. Keep in mind that Japan may very well be the only Asian country where bargaining, unless you're at a flea market (p172), is simply not done. While plastic is being accepted at more shops nowadays, it's a good idea to come armed with cold, hard cash. On luxury items like pricey electronics, the 5% VAT can be waived for foreigners, but you'll have to have your passport on you to take advantage of it.

Upscale shopping districts such as Ginza (p52) and Aoyama (p108) are good places to start for luxury items at fashion houses of international repute, including Chanel, Gucci or Mikimoto Pearl. If your stay is particularly short, hit Aoyama first – there's a good mix of international and Japanese heavyweights who've set up shop along Omote-sandō, and some of the architecture itself is as beautifully designed as the wares. Plus, the Harajuku backstreets (p108) adjacent to Aoyama complement the couture with Tokyo's famous street fashion. Takeshita-dōri is the best place to plunge in for an exploration of teenybopper culture. Ginza, on the other hand, has Tokyo's oldest, grand department stores, some of which have rooftop gardens and restaurant towns above and *depachika* (p57) below.

Other shopping districts around Central Tokyo include Jimbōchō, where bookshops trade in antique and rare books, as well as used books and manga. But a bigger scene for manga lies to the east of here in Akihabara, once famed (and still nicknamed for) its discount electronics.

Sprawling shopping malls that could each swallow several Southeast Asian villages whole include the older Sunshine City (p86) in Ikebukuro and the newer Roppongi Hills (p144). More intimate, human-scale shopping experiences can be sought in Daikanyama (p133) or Kichijōji (p92), where the smaller shops have their unique styles and sensibilities.

Even if shopping isn't your bag, any visitor to Tokyo should at least pop into Tōkyū Hands (p94), the 'Creative Life Store', which is sure to offer some captivating bauble to even the most consumption-averse. Shopping is leisure in this city, so come out to play and gain a little insight into the societal psyche in the bargain.

BEST SHOPS FOR OFFBEAT SOUVENIRS
> Don Quijote (p93)
> Kiddyland (p110)
> Kite Museum (p49)
> Meguro Parasitological Museum (p132)
> Tōkyū Hands (p94)

BEST TRADITIONAL HANDICRAFTS
> Bingoya (p95)
> Hashi Ginza Natsuno (p54)
> Japan Traditional Crafts Center (p85)
> Kamawanu (p134)
> Takumi Handicrafts (p57)

BEST PLACES TO FIND WASHI
> Haibara (p52)
> Itōya (p54)
> Sekaido (p94)

Opposite Temptations behind the glass in the shopping Mecca of Harajuku

SPECTATOR SPORTS

No sport in Japan is more popular than baseball, and the Tokyo area is home to no fewer than six of the country's 12 professional teams. The most popular team in Japan, the Yomiuri Giants, is based out of Tokyo Dome (also known as the 'Big Egg'). Tokyo Dome is probably the best place in town to catch a game, where fan clubs cheerleaders dressed in *happi* (half-coats) lead thousands of fans in synchronised cheers and singing. Beer girls with minikegs strapped to their backs run up and down the steep aisles pouring brews to customers while a small dirigible floats around the inside of the dome filming the action. In fair weather, however, it's equally enjoyable to take in a game at the outdoor Jingū Stadium, home of the Yakult Swallows. Baseball season begins at the end of March or the first week of April and runs until October.

Of course, besides the big two of baseball and *sumō* (p10), martial-arts events and smaller-scale sports competitions occur year-round. Check **Metropolis** (www.metropolis.co.jp) for extensive listings on current events.

BEST (ONLY) PLACE TO WATCH SUMŌ
> Ryōgoku Kokugikan (p64)

BEST STADIUM FOR J-LEAGUE SOCCER
> National Stadium (p117)

BEST BASEBALL STADIUM
> Tokyo Dome (p64)
> Jingū Stadium (p117)

Get on board during rush hour at Ueno Station

BACKGROUND
HISTORY
THE EARLY YEARS

Around the mid-15th century, a poet named Dōkan Ōta constructed Edo's first castle on the site of an old fortress. When Portuguese traders first set eyes on 16th-century Edo, it was little more than an outpost for aristocrats and monks who had fled a civil war in Kyoto. Within three centuries Edo would oust Kyoto as Japan's traditional seat of imperial power – and Tokyo would be born.

TOKUGAWA EDO

The father to this upstart child was the wily, madly ambitious shōgun, Ieyasu Tokugawa. His appointment by the emperor in 1603 was to change the fate of Tokyo (and Japan) forever.

A political survivor, Tokugawa knew he must divide and conquer his political foes. In a masterstroke, he forced all *daimyō* (feudal lords) throughout Japan to spend at least one year of every two in Edo. This policy of dislocation made it difficult for ambitious *daimyō* to usurp the Tokugawas.

Tokugawa systematically created a rigidly hierarchical society, comprising, in descending order: nobility; *daimyō* and their samurai; farmers; and finally artisans and merchants. Class dress, living quarters and even manner of speech were strictly codified. Class advancement was prohibited, though one could always, terrifyingly, descend to the underclasses, to the 'nonhuman' *hinin* and to *eta,* the untouchable class.

ISOLATION

After Ieyasu Tokugawa's death in 1616, his grandson Iemitsu Tokugawa, fearing Christian power, closed the country's borders in 1638. Japan was effectively removed from the world stage for nearly 300 years.

By the early 17th century, Edo (population over one million) was the largest city on earth. Its castelike society divided Edo into the *daimyō* high city (Yamanote) and a low working-class city (Shitamachi). Destructive fires often swept through its shantytowns. The locals christened these fires 'Edo-no-hana' ('flowers of Edo'). The cocky bravura of the expression sums up the tough Shitamachi spirit, still to be found in the backstreets of Ueno and Asakusa.

TOKYO RISING

When US Commodore Matthew Perry's armada of 'black ships' entered Edo (Tokyo) Bay demanding 'free trade' in 1853, despite spirited resistance from 2000 Tokugawa loyalists at the brief Battle of Ueno, the shōgunate fell apart and power reverted to Tokyo.

The Meiji Restoration refers to this consequent return of power to the emperor; however, Emperor Meiji's rule was more revolution than restoration. A crash course in industrialisation and militarisation began and by 1889 Japan had adopted a Western-style constitution – and Western-style empire building.

Nowhere was revolutionary change more evident than on the streets of the country's new capital city. Job-seekers flocked from tne country and Tokyo boomed.

CATASTROPHE & WAR

The Great Kantō Earthquake struck the boom town at noon on 1 September 1923. The subsequent fires, lasting some 40 hours, laid waste to the city. Although 142,000 lost their lives, worse was to come.

From the accession of Emperor Hirohito in 1926, nationalist fervour gripped the government. In 1931 the Japanese army invaded Manchuria, then China. By 1940 a pact with Germany and Italy had been signed and 'Greater Asia Co-Prosperity Sphere' was touted as the new order. On 7 December 1941 the Japanese attacked Pearl Harbor.

WWII was catastrophic for Tokyo. Incendiary bombing of the mostly wooden city commenced in March 1944. On the nights of 9 and 10 March 1945, 40% of the city was engulfed in a terrible firestorm and between 70,000 and 80,000 perished. By the time Emperor Hirohito made his famous address to the Japanese people on 15 August 1945, much of Tokyo was a wasteland.

BUBBLE & BUST

Tokyo rose phoenixlike from the ashes of WWII, and the economy flourished as almost no other in history. Ironically, it was sparked by US involvement in the neighbouring Korean War. The 1960s, '70s and early '80s saw unprecedented growth. Japan was suddenly an economic superpower – incredibly wealthy, globally powerful and omnipotent.

And then, suddenly, it wasn't. Japan's 'bubble economy' of the '80s floated ever higher on the strength of its technology and automobile exports. Emboldened by the belief that the bullish stock market and climbing property values would continue to rise, investors financed all manner of huge developments and projects. But this growth was unsustainable, and the burst of the bubble threw Japan into a recession from which it is still recovering.

But the cracks ran deeper than the fiscal fault lines. The Kōbe earthquake of January 1995 shook not only that city but the nation's confidence in the government's ability to respond quickly and effectively to such a monumental disaster. In March 1995, when members of the Aum Shinrikyō cult released sarin nerve gas on a crowded Tokyo commuter train, killing 12 and injuring 5000, Japan's self-belief took a severe blow.

TOKYO TODAY
While Japan's population greys and the birth rate declines, Tokyo continues to rev along at a youthful pace. As the age gap between generations keeps widening, so does anxiety about who will support the aging population in the decades to come. But for now, anxiety is not the first word that comes to mind in describing the entrepreneurial spirit, the relative openness to doing things in new ways and the attitudes of a younger generation who never knew life in the 'bubble era'.

LIFE AS A TOKYOITE
The life of the average Japanese citizen is bound by a massive network of obligation and counter-obligation to family, colleagues, the guy next door, ancestors who passed away generations ago – the list is endless. Those individuals who just can't stand it flee to Tokyo. The anonymity of the megalopolis is a magnet for misfits, rebels, artists and all the famous 'nails that stand out' (and duly get bashed down) in mainstream Japanese society. Thus it is, in many senses, the most liberated of Japanese cities. People scarcely know their neighbours, or care to.

With the disintegration of the family and continuing economic lethargy, the times they are a-changing. The generation gap between conventional, self-sacrificing parent and pierced, part-time-employee child has never been greater. Younger people who were born after the bubble era are not hampered so much by the conventions of that time, and are more open to creativity and experimentation. Career adjustments – like bouncing back from losing a job – come more naturally to the younger generation. Old systems and cultural attitudes are slow to change, but the societal flux is probably most apparent and dynamic in Tokyo.

ETIQUETTE

Given Tokyo's distinctly different place in Japanese society, it's difficult to offend. Moreover, Japanese people are highly forgiving of foreign visitors' minor social gaffes. But there are a few rules of etiquette that must always be followed. When entering a house or any tatami (woven-floor matting) room, always take off your shoes. If in doubt, do as everyone else does. It's considered rude (and disgusting) to blow your nose in public – maintain a stoic and noisy sniffle until you find a private place. Except for ice cream, eating while walking down the street is also just not done.

For those in Tokyo on business, *meishi* (business cards) carry a lot of weight in society and are ritually exchanged on first meetings. Politely accept – or offer – a card with both hands and examine it before putting it away, and don't write on a card that someone has given you.

And when invited to someone's home, bring a small gift that's presented attractively – an occasion for requesting the elaborate wrapping available when you make your purchase. As with *meishi,* offer the gift with both hands and a slight bow, and expect it to be politely refused a few times before you insist they accept it.

GOVERNMENT & POLITICS
THE CHRYSANTHEMUM THRONE

In September 2006 Princess Kiko (wife of Prince Akishino, second in line to the throne after Crown Prince Naruhito) gave birth to the first male heir to the Japanese throne in over 40 years. Man-on-the-street TV interviews showed the emotional reactions of Tokyoites to this momentous news. Although Emperor Akihito and Empress Michiko are but figureheads, the Imperial Family is still very much revered and deeply respected in Japan. This outpouring of happiness also coincided with a sudden – though not unexpected – tapering-off of the controversy that marked the years before the new prince was born.

Increasingly intense debate had been growing about changing the Japanese constitution to allow a female heir to ascend the Chrysanthemum Throne. The Crown Prince Naruhito and Crown Princess Masako have only a daughter. And while recent polls showed that 76% of the general population supported the idea of female ascendancy, conservative elements in branches of the imperial family and Japan's governing body, the Diet, staunchly oppose it on the grounds that a female heir would break the traditional male lineage. The debate remains open, but for the moment Prince Hisahito's birth has significantly lessened its urgency.

Unfortunately, the pressure to have a son – coupled with the isolated life inside the Imperial Palace – has had a deleterious effect on Crown Princess Masako, once a promising young diplomat. Two years after the birth of her daughter, Princess Aiko, in 2001, she largely withdrew from public life, though of late she has begun making more frequent public appearances. It remains to be seen what the future will hold for young Princess Aiko, as times change and traditional restrictions do not.

THE RULING DIET

The governing body, known as the Diet, is based here in the capital and is made up of two houses. The party controlling the majority of seats in the Diet is the ruling party and has the right to appoint the prime minister. Since its inception in 1955, the conservative Liberal Democratic Party (LDP) has controlled the Diet, barring a few years during the mid '90s.

In theory, Japan is a democratic country, with members of the Diet elected by popular vote. However, in practice, real power is held by powerful political cliques descended from generations of the nation's elite, who are allied with Japan's dominant *keiretsu* (business cartels). Until relatively recently, this seemed to suit Japanese voters just fine, but a recession plus structural reforms by former prime minister Junichirō Koizumi stoked more political fire among the populace.

Since Koizumi's resignation in 2006, the office of the PM has had a revolving door, with Shinzo Abe succeeding him for one year and Yasuo Fukuda following suit for another. In autumn 2008, Taro Aso was appointed by the LDP but lost the confidence of the nation with gaffes such as misreading kanji in speeches and offending the elderly population with insensitive comments about their value to society, all while a recession took hold. The LDP's grip on the Diet may be weakening; watch this space.

ECONOMY

With the world's second-largest GDP, Japan's economy is just behind that of the USA – though that hasn't meant easy street for Japan these past two decades. The country is still feeling, though no longer reeling from, the effects of the 'bubble economy' bursting in the early '80s. The

WORKING STIFFS

The Japanese love incorporating foreign words into their vocabulary; here are a few examples of local lingo for naming that employee.

> Salarymen – These are the guys in suits of sombre colours, often with a matching dour demeanour. But, after staying late at work to keep up appearances, they're often found red-faced and slap-happy at their favourite *izakaya* (pub-eatery) as they booze with their colleagues.

> OLs – Short for 'office ladies' – they may do the same work as salarymen but receive appallingly less pay. Others might be secretaries biding their time before they can marry a salaryman, quit the office job and take up recreational shopping. OLs often travel in packs, dressed in matching corporate vest-and-skirt combos.

> Freeters – A combination of 'freelance' and '*arbeiter*' ('worker' in German), these are the young people handing out advert-emblazoned packs of tissues on the streets or working that convenience-store register. They pick up work when they need it, and drop it when they don't.

Asiawide financial collapse, ineffectual government response and tough competition from the USA were all key contributing factors, and the resulting recession lasted well into the '90s and early 2000s.

However, the bright side of those darker financial days is that the economic slump inspired – or forced – businesspeople to reassess the traditional career arc that meant a lifetime allegiance to one's company. The concept of a job for life is no longer taken for granted, nor necessarily desired, by the younger generation. Part-time and casual employment are on the rise, with younger people working merely to make a living, and living more alternatively than their elders. Occasionally 'parasite singles' are blamed for the sluggish economy, with economic experts claiming that they should be buying property instead of living with (and mooching off) their parents. But unemployment hovered at a respectable 3.9% over 2008.

For visitors, the levelling-off of Japan's economy means a more even playing field for travellers to stretch their yen a little further.

ENVIRONMENT

On a fundamental geographical level, Japan is part of the Pacific 'Ring of Fire', the tectonic activity of which created the majestic conical shape of Mt Fuji and crumbled the city of Kōbe in 1995. Although minor earthquakes occur all the time, there's no telling when the next big one

BAG IT

The straightforward request that your purchase not be bagged may be met with some confusion, but environmental awareness is growing in Tokyo. The tradition of wrapping every single solitary purchase is an art bordering on obsession in Japan, where even the humblest of items – a pastry, for example – is wrapped in plastic before being wrapped in paper before then being placed reverentially into a bag with handles (prominently displaying a status-bearing logo, for luxury items).

You can cut down on the plague of bags by saying, *'Fukuro wa iranai desu'* ('I don't need a bag').

will strike. There's little point in paranoia, but it pays to note where exits are located.

On a more human level, Japan's limited land mass plus its dense population equals an environmental quandary. Consequently, Tokyo's garbage collection services are quite strict about adhering to their own stringent regulations, which require the separation of burnable, non-burnable and recyclable refuse. If it's not properly separated before being left out for pickup, it's simply not picked up. There's still too much plastic packaging in use in the first place, but you can do your small part by cutting back on plastic-bag consumption (see above).

Vending machines, convenience stores and some train stations usually have recycling receptacles clearly marked, but there's a distinct lack of rubbish receptacles around Tokyo in general.

THE ARTS
FILM

Akira Kurosawa, the most famous director of Japanese cinema's golden era, brought Japanese film into the spotlight when his *Rashōmon* (1950) took top prize at the Venice Film Festival. Illustrious filmmakers who followed include Shohei Imamura, who examines human behaviour with a piercing eye in works such as *The Profound Desire of the Gods* (1968) and Oshima Nagisa's *Ai no Corrida* (In the Realm of the Senses), a tale of an obsessive love that was banned in many countries when it was released in 1976.

More contemporary films include Jūzō Itami's *Tampopo* (1985), a characteristically quirky comedy about sex and food, and the award-winning *Zatoichi* (2003), featuring actor-director Takeshi 'Beat' Kitano as a blind swordsman. Japan's gorgeous *anime* gems, such as Hayao Miyazaki's *Spir-*

ited Away (2001), continue to issue from Tokyo onto international screens. More recent works include the brilliant but a tad depressing *Dare mo Shiranai* (2004) by Hirokazu Koreeda, based on the true story about a wayward mother who abandoned her four children in an apartment in Tokyo.

LITERATURE
Often with a surrealist edge or a dose of magical realism, Japanese contemporary literature – much of which is written by authors who've spent most of their lives in Tokyo – provides a perspective on the more elusive emotional side of life in the city. Nobel Laureate Kenzaburo Ōe's clear-eyed *A Personal Matter* tells the story of a man faced with a conflict of freedom and responsibility that transcends Japanese social mores. A departure from his more surrealist work, Haruki Murakami's celebrated *Norwegian Wood* chronicles the coming of age of a university student in late-1960s Japan. And for lighter, but surprisingly solid fare, pick up *Kitchen* (1998) by Banana Yoshimoto; seemingly superficial themes of food, pop culture and unconventional sexuality speak to an immediate sort of urban existentialism.

MUSIC
Live gigs rock the 'live houses' every night of the week in Tokyo's basement bars, mostly on the city's west side. You name it, someone makes or hosts it – from Japanese hip-hop and punk rock to acid jazz.

Japan has an enormous domestic record market, and Tokyo is very much a part of the international live-music circuit. Many top performers, from every genre of contemporary and classical music, book shows here. Along with Tokyo's better-known exports, such as composer Ryūichi Sakamoto and food-fetish rockers Shonen Knife, are musical collage artists Buffalo Daughter, and postmodern mixmaster Cornelius, who overlays samples of birdsong with harmonic vocal tracks, guitar and synthesized beats. Veteran DJ Takkyu Ishino packs 'em in, while bands like Dragon Ash and Kreva bring a Japanese flavour to hip-hop and reggae.

Tokyo mainstream consists significantly of *aidoru* (idol singers) and girl- or boy-bands, manufactured J-pop confections sweetened to perfection for mass marketing. Don't overindulge, or you'll get a toothache.

PERFORMANCE ARTS
Kabuki, *nō* (classical Japanese drama), and bunraku (puppet theatre) are well represented throughout the city, with several theatres featuring

regular performances. *Taiko* (traditional Japanese drumming) is where music meets martial art and mysticism.

Tokyo is also a centre for Japan's enigmatic, challenging modern dance form, *butō*. Its bizarre movements, weird lighting, and long periods of inaction are not everyone's cup of *o-cha* (green tea), but most certainly memorable. Check with a tourist-information centre (p202), or local listings for current performances. Seek out Dairakudakan (www.dairakudakan.com), Sankaijuku (www.sankaijuku.com), or most powerful of all, Taihen (www.ne.jp/asahi/imaju/taihen), whose members are all severely physically disabled.

VISUAL ART

Tokyo's contemporary-art scene is thriving. Its galleries possess a lack of pretension that is startlingly refreshing – it's easy to walk into a show and start a conversation with the artists themselves. Progressive spaces all over town give space to exciting work, much of it by the talented young artists of the city's prestigious art colleges.

Bigger museums tend to go for heavy-hitting names: Rodin, Renoir, Da Vinci, Degas. The superstars of Western art are most-oft found at the National Museum of Western Art (p68). But don't be surprised if they pop up, along with their Japanese counterparts, in the department-store galleries dotted around town. The greatest concentration of small galleries – with roughly 400 exhibition spaces – clusters in Ginza (p45).

DIRECTORY
TRANSPORT
ARRIVAL & DEPARTURE
AIR

Narita Airport

Tokyo's main international airport is **Narita International Airport** (www .narita-airport.jp/en), 66km from the city. When flying out of Narita, be sure to check which terminal your airline departs from, as the distance between the two is significant enough to warrant separate train stops.

Information

Flight information (☎ 0476-348 000,
General inquiries (☎ 0476-322 802)
Air Canada (☎ 5405 8800; www.aircanada.ca)
Air France (☎ 3570 8577; www.airfrance .com)
American Airlines (☎ 4550 2111; www.aa .com)
ANA (☎ 0120-029 709; www.ana.co.jp/eng)

British Airways (☎ 3570 8657; www.ba.com)
Cathay Pacific Airways (☎ 5159 1700; www.cathaypacific.com)
Japan Airlines (www.jal.co.jp/en)
KLM (☎ 3570 8770; www.klm.com)
Korean Air (☎ 0476-327 561; www.korean air.com)
Lufthansa (☎ 4333 7655)
Qantas Airways (☎ 3593 7000; www.qantas .com.au)
United Airlines (☎ 3817 4411; www.ual .com)
Virgin Atlantic Airways (☎ 3499 8811; www.virgin-atlantic.com)

Airport Access

Train N'EX (JR Narita Express) runs to Tokyo Station (¥2940, 53 minutes), Shinjuku Station (¥3110, 1½ hours), Ikebukuro Station (¥3110, one hour and 40 minutes) and Yokohama Station (¥4180, 1½ hours). Airport Narita Kaisoku (rapid service) also goes to Tokyo station (¥1280, 1½ hours). Keisei Skyliner goes to Ueno (¥1920, 56 minutes). The private Keisei line also runs a Tokkyū (limited express; ¥1000, one hour and 11 minutes) service.
Bus Limousine Buses (www.limousinebus .co.jp/en/) connect Narita with central Tokyo

CLIMATE CHANGE & TRAVEL

Travel – especially air travel – is a significant contributor to global climate change. At Lonely Planet, we believe that all who travel have a responsibility to limit their personal impact. As a result, we have teamed with Rough Guides and other concerned industry partners to support Climate Care, which allows people to offset the greenhouse gases they are responsible for with contributions to energy-saving projects and other climate-friendly initiatives in the developing world. Lonely Planet offsets all staff and author travel.

For more information, turn to the responsible travel pages on www.lonelyplanet .com. For details on offsetting your carbon emissions and a carbon calculator, go to www .climatecare.org.

STAY AWHILE

Short city breaks make great getaways, but air travel is a becoming a devastating contributor to global warming. What can you do to lessen the impact? Why not take a longer holiday? If a few days in Tokyo has given you a taste of the city in all its beautifully bizarre and uniquely Japanese glory, consider making your next trip a longer one: take a day trip out to the lovely mountain resort town of Hakone near Mt Fuji, or to the temples, shrines and Great Buddha statue in Kamakura. Or go even further and travel across Japan using its world-class rail system.

(¥3100; 1½ hours), making stops directly at many major hotels around the city, among them the Cerulean Tower Tōkyū Hotel in Shibuya, Keiō Plaza Hotel in Shinjuku, Marunouchi Hotel in Central Tokyo and ANA Intercontinental in Akasaka.
Taxis From Tokyo to Narita airport will cost about ¥30,000; travel times vary widely depending on traffic.

Haneda Airport
While the vast majority arrive at Narita International Airport, a few international flights operate through Haneda Airport near central Tokyo.

Information
General inquiries & flight information
(☎ 5757 8111; (www.tokyo-airport-bldg .co.jp/en)

Airport Access
Train The Tokyo Monorail (www.tokyo-mono rail.co.jp/english/) is a great way to get to and from Haneda. The monorail connects each terminal at Haneda with Hamamatsuchō Station on the JR Yamanote line (¥470, 20 minutes). You can then easily catch a Yamanote line train to your final destination. Purchase tickets at the station vending machines, which have an English option.
Bus Limousine buses (www.limousinebus.co .jp/en/) run between Haneda and various points around Tokyo, including Tokyo Station and Shinjuku Station (¥1300 to ¥1600, one hour). Purchase your ticket at the counters on the arrival floor of each terminal; bus stops are directly outside the 2nd floor of each terminal.
Taxis A trip between Haneda and Tokyo station costs around ¥7000.

TRAIN
Japan Railways' (JR) famed *shinkansen* (bullet trains) serve Northern Honshū, Central and Western Japan and Kyūshū. The slower, less expensive *tokkyū* (limited express), *kyūko* (express) and *futsū* (ordinary) are options on every route between cities; however, not many people use them for long-distance travel. One-way, reserved-seat *shinkansen* fares for *nozomi* trains (which make the fewest stops) are ¥13,720 from Kyoto to Tokyo, ¥22,520 from Fukuoka to Tokyo, and ¥14,250 from Osaka to Tokyo. The main terminals are Tokyo (Map pp46–7, E5) and Ueno (Map p67, C4) stations.

Private lines running from stations on the Yamanote line are the quickest, cheapest bet to Kamakura, Mt Fuji, Hakone and Yokohama. They connect to Shinjuku (Map p89, B4) and Shibuya (Map p119, C4) stations. The Tōbu line for Nikkō runs from Asakusa Station (Map p75, C3).

BUS

Domestic long-distance buses mainly arrive at Tokyo Station's Highway Bus Terminal (Map pp46–7, E5) near the Yaesu south exit. Highway buses also depart from the west side of Shinjuku Station (Map p89, B4). Services to both Osaka and Kyoto are operated by JR (☎ 3844 1950); you can buy tickets from a Green Window office at most larger JR train stations.

VISA

Citizens of 62 countries, including Singapore, Hong Kong, Korea, Canada, USA, Australia, New Zealand, UK, France, Germany, the Netherlands and Sweden, do not require visas to enter Japan for stays of 90 days or fewer. Consult www.mofa.go.jp/j_info/visit/visa/02.html for a complete list of visa-exempt countries.

GETTING AROUND

Short-term visitors and long-term residents alike mainly use the city's excellent subway system and the JR train lines, especially the JR Yamanote line. It rings the inner city making almost everywhere accessible in under an hour. All stations have signposts and maps in English. The Tokyo Metro (www.tokyometro.jp) subway lines are colour coded, and regular English signposting makes the system easy to use. The train and subway services in Tokyo are famed for their punctuality, and trains are frequent. Nearest stations are

ELUSIVE ADDRESSES

In Tokyo, finding a place by address alone is challenging at best, even for locals. Apart from *dōri* (main roads), very few streets have names – addresses indicate their locations in relation to their larger contexts. So, for example, an address listed as 1-11-2 Ginza, Chūō-ku in this book means that the place is in Tokyo's Chūō ward, in Ginza's 1-*chōme* (an area consisting of several blocks), in block 11, in building 2 of that block.

Chōme, blocks and building numbers aren't necessarily located in a logical order, so it's best to use a map (the bilingual *Tokyo City Atlas*, published by Kodansha, is invaluable if you'll be spending much time in Tokyo). Most establishments print simple maps on their business cards. Another effective way to find your way is to stop at a *kōban* (police box) in the area, where the friendly neighbourhood police spend much of their time giving directions.

listed after the 🚃 (for the Yamanote and above-ground lines) and 🚇 (for subway lines) in listings.

TRAVEL PASSES

The Tokyo Combination Ticket day pass can be used on all JR, subway and bus lines within the Tokyo metropolitan area. It costs ¥1580 (¥790 for children aged six to 11) and is available from station offices in most JR stations and major subway hubs like Ginza, Nihombashi and Shinjuku.

Longer-stay visitors should consider purchasing a Pasmo or Suica card, both of which can be used on both JR, Tokyo Metro subway lines, and several other rail lines in Tokyo. Both cards circumvent the hassle of puzzling over transfers, as they automatically calculate your fare each time you pass through a station wicket.

Pasmo cards are sold at ticket-vending machines in most subway stations in denominations of ¥1000, ¥3000 and ¥5000. Suica cards can be purchased at JR ticket windows with a ¥500 deposit. Suica cards can be topped up at JR ticket-vending machines.

TRAIN

Tokyo is serviced by a combination of JR, private inner-city subway lines and private suburban

lines. Trains run from around 5am to midnight. The JR Yamanote line is augmented by the Chūō and Sōbu lines. Fares begin at ¥130, and the green maps above ticket-vending machines have fares clearly marked. If maps do not include English, simply buy the minimum fare and pay the balance at a fare-adjustment machine at your destination. For train information, call the **JR English information line** (☎ 050-2016 1603; 🕐 10am-6pm Mon-Fri).

SUBWAY

There are 13 subway lines, nine of which are TRTA lines (fares start at ¥160) and four of which are TOEI lines (fares start at ¥170). Services on the two systems are essentially the same, and connections are seamless except for the fact that they have separate ticketing systems.

Ticket-vending machines that operate in English are available at every station. If you can't work out how much your fare will be, buy the cheapest ticket and pay the difference at a fare-adjustment machine at your destination. Services run from around 5.30am to midnight.

TAXI

Rates start at ¥710 per 2km, then the meter rises by ¥90 every 300m or so. There's a 20% late-night sur-

Recommended Subway Routes

	To Ginza	To Shinjuku	To Shibuya	To Roppongi	To Asakusa
From Ginza	n/a	Marunouchi line (16mins)	Ginza line (15mins)	Hibiya line (10mins)	Ginza line (17mins)
From Shinjuku	Marunouchi line (16mins)	n/a	JR Yamanote line (7mins)	Toei Ōedo line (9mins)	Marunouchi line to Akasaka-mitsuke, transfer to Ginza line (34mins)
From Shibuya	Ginza line (15mins)	JR Yamanote line (7mins)	n/a	Hanzōmon line to Aoyama-itchōme, transfer to Toei Ōedo line (12mins)	Ginza line (32mins)
From Roppongi	Hibiya line (10mins)	Toei Ōedo line (9mins)	Toei Ōedo line to Aoyama-itchōme, transfer to Hanzōmon line (12mins)	n/a	Toei Ōedo line to Daimon, transfer to Toei Asakusa line (28mins)
From Asakusa	Ginza line (17mins)	Ginza line to Akasaka-mitsuke, transfer to Marunouchi line	Ginza line (32mins)	Toei Asakusa line to Daimon, transfer to Toei Ōedo line (28mins)	n/a

charge applied to fares between 10pm and 5am. You'll also rack up about ¥100 every two minutes you spend in a typical Tokyo traffic jam.

Taxi vacancy is indicated by a red light; a green light means there's a night-time surcharge and a yellow light means that the cab is on call. Watch out for the automatic doors on taxis; they'll magically close themselves when you get in or out. Taxi drivers can plug a venue's telephone number into their GPS system to find its location.

CAR & MOTORCYCLE
On a short trip to Tokyo you're unlikely to need or want your own wheels, what with Tokyo's outstanding rail system and miserable traffic congestion. However, if you do need to hire a vehicle, be sure to obtain an International Driving Permit before you arrive in Japan as well as bringing a driver's licence from your own country.

Typical rates for small cars are ¥8000 or ¥9000 for the first day, and ¥5500 to ¥7000 each day thereafter. On top of this there is a ¥1000-per-day insurance fee. Mileage is usually unlimited.

We recommend the following:
Mazda Rent-a-Lease (☎ 5286 0740)
Nippon Rent-a-Car (☎ 3485 7196)
Toyota Rent-a-Lease (☎ 3264 0100)

BOAT

Water buses are a great way to see a different slice of Tokyo, either as a short tour or as a relaxing means of getting around. **Suijo Bus** (Map p75, C4; ☎ 3841 9178; www.suijobus .co.jp/english/index.html; Azumabashi-mae, Asakusa, Taitō-ku; from ¥720; ⏱ 9.55am-7.10pm, hours vary seasonally; Ⓜ Ginza & Toei Asakusa lines to Asakusa, (exits 4 & A5)) lines can shuttle you from Asakusa to Central Tokyo and on again to Odaiba.

PRACTICALITIES
BUSINESS HOURS

Banks 9am-3pm or 5pm Mon-Fri, closed national holidays
Convenience stores 24hr
Museums 9.30am-4.30pm
Offices 9am-5pm Mon-Fri (some open Sat am)
Post offices 9am-5pm Mon-Fri (major post offices 8am-8pm)
Public offices 9am-noon & 1-5pm Mon-Fri
Restaurants 11.30am-2.30pm & 6-10.30pm (family-run restaurants open from 11.30am-11.30pm)
Shops 10am-8pm

CLIMATE & WHEN TO GO

Spring (March to May) and Autumn (September to November) are the most balmy seasons. Typhoons usually occur in September and October. Summers are hot and humid, with temperatures getting into the

GOOD THINGS TO KNOW

> Electricity – 100V 50Hz AC, two-pronged flat-pin plugs.
> Metric System – Japan uses the international metric system.
> Newspapers & Magazines – *The Japan Times*, *Daily Yomiuri* and the *Asahi/International Herald Tribune* are English-language newspapers available at newsstands in or near train stations. *Tokyo Journal* is a good events magazine sold in bookstores, and the free *Metropolis* is an excellent, intelligent weekly magazine available every Friday at cafés and bookstores around Tokyo.
> Radio – InterFM on 76.1FM broadcasts news and daily-life information mainly in English, and in seven other languages, including Spanish and Chinese.
> Time – Japan is nine hours ahead of Greenwich Mean Time (GMT). Daylight-saving time is not used in Japan.
> TV – NHK is the government-run TV station; its 7pm and 9pm reports are bilingual. CNN and BBC World Service are available in all major hotels.

high 30s. The *tsuyu* (rainy season), in June, means several weeks of torrential rain can wreak havoc with a tight travel itinerary. In winter the weather is good with mainly clear, sunny skies and the occasional snowfall. Avoid major holidays such as Golden Week (29 April to 5 May) and the mid-August O-bon festival. The city tends to close down over New Year (around 29 December to 6 January).

DISCOUNTS

In general, not many discounts are offered to sights in Tokyo. Most major sights offer discounts for children, and very young children may get in free. An international student card will earn discounts on entry fees to many museums and prices on long-distance train travel. Seniors can get discounts to some major sights, and Japanese domestic airlines (JAS, JAL and ANA) offer senior discounts of about 25% on some flights. However, that's about the extent of it.

Prices are listed in this book in the following order: adult/student/child six to 12/child under six; typically, a listing like **$** ¥1000/500 refers to adult/child prices.

One excellent investment, if you'll be in Tokyo for awhile and plan to visit several museums, is the Grutt Pass (p71). The pass grants discounted or free entry to nearly 50 museums and zoos around Tokyo.

EMERGENCIES

Violent crime and theft, though they exist, are rare in Tokyo; that said, you should exercise the same awareness of your surroundings as you would anywhere else. Women should be aware of *chikan* (gropers) working crowded trains. Yelling '*Chikan!*' will often shame the offender into stopping, but look before you let loose – sometimes a crowded train is just a crowded train.

Although most emergency operators in Tokyo don't speak English, they will immediately refer you to someone who does. For free English assistance or advice, you can also call the **Japan Helpline** (☎ 0120-461 997; ☽ 24hr), or the **Tokyo English Life Line** (☎ 5774 0992; www.telljp.com; ☽ 9am-11pm).

Other useful numbers:
Ambulance ☎ 119
Fire ☎ 119
Police ☎ 110

HEALTH

All hospitals listed here have English-speaking staff and 24-hour accident and emergency departments. Travel insurance is advisable to cover any medical treatment you may need while in Tokyo. Medical treatment is among the best in the world, but also the most expensive. Note also that you will be expected to pay in full for treatment or provide sufficient proof that your insurance company will cover the payment.

We recommend the following:
Japanese Red Cross Medical Center (Nihon Sekijūjisha Iryō Sentā; Map pp140-1, B6; ☎ 3400 1311; www.med.jrc.or.jp in Japanese; 4-1-22 Hiro-o, Shibuya-ku; ⊕ Hibiya line to Hiro-o, exits 1 & 2)
St Luke's International Hospital (Seiroka Byōin; Map pp46-7, F7; ☎ 3541 5151; www.luke.or.jp; 9-1 Akashichō, Chūō-ku; ⊕ Hibiya line to Tsukiji, exits 3 & 4)
Tokyo Medical & Surgical Clinic (Map pp140-1, G6; ☎ 3436 3028; www.tmsc.jp; 2F, 32 Shiba-kōen Bldg, 3-4-30 Shiba-kōen, Minato-ku; ⊕ Toei Mita line to Onarimon, exit A1)

PHARMACIES

Pharmacies are easy to find and some have Japanese-English symptom charts. Staff speaks English at the listed pharmacies:
American Pharmacy (Map pp46-7, D5; ☎ 5220-7716; B1F, Marunouchi Bldg, 2-4-1 Marunouchi, Chiyoda-ku; ⊙ 9am-9pm Mon-Fri, 10am-9pm Sat, 10am-8pm Sun; ⊕ Marunouchi line to Tokyo, exit 4)
National Azabu Supermarket (Map pp140-1; ☎ 3442 3181; 4-5-2 Minami-Azabu, Minato-ku; ⊙ 9.30am-7pm; ⊕ Hibiya line to Hiro-o, exits 1 & 2).

HOLIDAYS

When a public holiday falls on a Sunday, the following Monday is taken as a holiday. If a business remains open on a holiday, it will usually be closed the following day.
New Year's Day 1 January
Coming-of-Age Day 2nd Monday in January
National Foundation Day 11 February
Spring Equinox Day 21 March
Green Day 29 April
Constitution Day 3 May
Children's Day 5 May
Marine Day 3rd Monday in July
Respect-for-the-Aged Day 3rd Monday in September
Autumn Equinox Day 23 September
Sports Day 2nd Monday in October
Culture Day 3 November
Labour Thanksgiving Day 23 November
Emperor's Birthday 23 December

INFORMATION & ORGANISATIONS

Contact the **Japanese Red Cross Language Service Volunteers** (Map pp140-1, H5; ☎ 3438 1311; http://accessible.jp.org/tokyo/en; 1-1-3 Shiba Daimon, Minato-ku) to get a copy of its indispensable *Accessible Tokyo* guide, or peruse the website for the same detailed, current information on getting around Tokyo.

INTERNET
ACCESS

Internet access is rapidly improving. Some bars and cafés offer net access and/or wi-fi for free – check out **Freespot** (www.freespot.com/users/map_e.html) for locations near you. The **Apple Store** (Map pp46-7; ☎ 5159 8200; 3-5-12 Ginza, Chūō-ku; admission free; ⊙ 10am-9pm;

🚇 Ginza & Hibiya lines to Ginza, exits A9 & A13) in Ginza is a good place for a quick stop. Many midrange hotels and most top-end hotels offer in-room LAN access, though you may be charged a usage fee.

Alternatively, you could do as the Tokyoites do and head to one of the *manga kissa* (p100) around town.

Recommend:

Aprecio (Map p89, C2; ☎ 3205 7336; www .aprecio.co.jp in Japanese; B1F, Hygeia Plaza, 2-44-1 Kabukichō, Shinjuku-ku; 1st 30min ¥300, 10min thereafter ¥100; ⏰ 24hr; 🚃 JR Yamanote line to Shinjuku, east exit) This clean, comfortable spot in Kabukichō offers all the usuals in smoking and nonsmoking wings, and has massage and beauty services, billiards and darts.

Bagus Gran Cyber Cafe (Map p119, B3; ☎ 5428 3676; www.bagus-99.com/netcafe in Japanese; 6F, 28-6 Udagawachō, Shibuya-ku; 8 hours ¥1500; ⏰ 24hr; 🚃 JR Yamanote line to Shibuya, Hachikō exit) This popular chain has branches all over Tokyo.

USEFUL WEBSITES

The LP website (www.lonelyplanet.com) offers a speedy link to many of Tokyo's websites. Other excellent sites include the following:

Metropolis (http://metropolis.co.jp)
Superfuture (www.superfuture.com/super travel/supercity/1)
Tokyo Food Page (www.bento.com/tokyo food.html)
Tokyo Journal (www.tokyo.to)
Tokyo Qool (http://tokyoq.com)

LANGUAGE

Note: Letters in square brackets are not pronounced.

BASICS

Hello.	*konnichiwa.*
Goodbye.	*sayonara.*
How are you?	*o-genki des[u]. ka?*
I'm fine.	*genki des[u].*
Excuse me.	*sumimasen.*
Yes.	*hai.*
No.	*iie.*
Thanks.	*dōmo (arigatō).*
You're welcome.	*dō itashimashite.*
Do you speak English?	*eigo ga hanase mas[u] ka?*
I don't understand.	*wakarimasen.*

EATING & DRINKING

That was delicious!	*oishikatta.*
I'm a vegetarian.	*watashi wa bejitarian des[u].*
Please bring the bill.	*(o-kanjō/o-aiso) o onegai shimas[u].*

Local dishes

kabayaki	skewers of grilled eel
katsu-don	fried pork cutlet with rice
okonomiyaki	Japanese-style pancake
tempura moriawase	a selection of tempura
zaru soba	cold buckwheat noodles with seaweed strips

SHOPPING

| How much is it? | ikura des[u] ka? |
| That's too expensive. | taka-sugi mas[u]. |

EMERGENCIES

I'm sick.	kibun ga warui des[u].
Help!	tas[u]kete!
Call the police.	keisatsu o yonde kudasai!
Call an ambulance.	kyūkyūsha o yonde.

DAYS & NUMBERS

today	kyō
tomorrow	ash[i]ta
yesterday	kinō
0	zero/rei
1	ichi
2	ni
3	san
4	yon/shi
5	go
6	roku
7	nana/shichi
8	hachi
9	kyū/ku
10	jū
11	jūichi
12	jūni
13	jūsan
14	jūyon/jūshi
20	nijū
21	nijūichi
30	sanjū
100	hyaku
1000	sen
10,000	man

MONEY

Despite its status as a top-tier, modern city, Tokyo still largely runs on a cash economy. Hotels and high-end restaurants will accept credit cards, but many less exclusive shops and services do not. Since it's generally safe to carry around large amounts of cash in Tokyo, line your pockets with some money just for walking around. You'll burn through yen quickly in Tokyo; if you're not on a tight budget, plan on spending a daily average of around ¥5000 to ¥8000 for meals, train fares and admission costs.

CURRENCY

The currency in Japan is the yen (¥). Coins come in denominations of ¥1, ¥5, ¥10, ¥50, ¥100 and ¥500; notes in denominations of ¥1000, ¥2000, ¥5000 and ¥10,000. Newer-issue ¥500 coins aren't accepted by some vending machines.

TRAVELLERS CHEQUES

There's little difference in commission charged by banks and big hotels. All major brands are acceptable, but cheques in yen or US dollars are preferred over other currencies.

CREDIT CARDS

Visa, MasterCard, Amex and Diners Club are widely accepted...where credit cards are accepted. For 24-

hour card cancellations or assistance, call these numbers:

Amex ☎ 0120-020 120
Diners Club ☎ 0120-074 024
JCB (☎ 0120-500 544
MasterCard (☎ 0053-111 3886
Visa (☎ 0053-111 1555)

ATMS

Tokyo post offices have ATMs that accept foreign-issued cards, 9am to 5pm Monday to Friday. If you're caught without cash after-hours, most 7-11 convenience stores have international ATMs. Citibank is your best bet for 24-hour ATMs that accept international cards; some Citibank ATM locations include Shinjuku, Ginza and Roppongi.

TELEPHONE

Local telephone calls cost ¥10 for the first three minutes, and then ¥10 for each minute thereafter. Phonecards are available from both newsstands and convenience stores starting in denominations of ¥500 and ¥1000 and are the most convenient way to call either locally or internationally.

Japan's mobile-phone network runs on the CDMA standard – incompatible with the widespread GSM system used in Europe, Australia and the rest of Asia (South Korea being the exception). However, several companies in Japan offer short-term mobile phone rentals at reasonable rates, from

around ¥3000 per week. Many even have pick-up and drop-off counters at Narita airport. Try one of the following:

DoCoMo (☎ 0120-680 100; www.mobile rental.jp/english/index.html)
GoMobile (☎ 5405 2298; www.gomobile .co.jp)
Pupuru (☎ 052-957 1801; www.pupuru.com)
Rentafone (☎ 0120-746 487; www.renta fonejapan.com)
Softbank (☎ 3560 7730; www.softbank -rental.jp)

COUNTRY & CITY CODES

Japan ☎ 81
Tokyo ☎ 03

USEFUL PHONE NUMBERS

International directory assistance ☎ 0057
International operator ☎ 0051
Local directory assistance ☎ 104
Reverse-charge (collect) ☎ 0051

TIPPING

Tipping is not standard practice in Japan. Expect to pay a service charge (10% to 20%) at upper-end restaurants and hotels.

TOILETS

Public toilets can be found everywhere, but the most luxurious are in the big department stores. They also tend to be high tech, outfitted with bidet, dryer and rushing-water sound effects to mask unseemly noise. Japanese-style squat toilets are also still an option at most public toilets.

TOURIST INFORMATION

JNTO Tokyo TIC (Map pp46-7, E6; ☎ 3201 3331; www.jnto.go.jp; 10F, Kōtsū Kaikan Bldg, 2-10-1 Yūraku-chō, Chiyoda-ku; ⊗ 9am-5pm; ℞ JR Yamanote line to Yūrakuchō) The JNTC provides excellent, up-to-date information on Tokyo and can make reservations for ryokan (Japanese inns).

Narita Airport TIC (☎ 0476-303 383, 0476-345 877; Terminals 1 & 2, Narita International Airport; ⊗ 8am-8pm) These TICs are located in both arrivals terminals and can help with hotel bookings.

Tokyo Tourist Information Center (Map p89, A3; ☎ 5321 3077; 1F, Tokyo Metropolitan Government Bldg No 1, 2-8-1 Nishi-Shinjuku, Shinjuku-ku; ⊗ 9.30am-6.30pm; Ⓣ Toei Ōedo line to Tochōmae, exit A4) A good place to pick up a Grutt Pass (¥2000; p71), free tourist map and information in English.

TRAVELLERS WITH DISABILITIES

Tokyo's size and complexity make it challenging for the mobility impaired, as well as the visually and hearing impaired. The upside is that attitudes to people with disabilities have vastly improved in the last two decades, and newer buildings tend to have excellent facilities. Advance planning is the key to a successful trip.

The ♿ icon throughout this guidebook denotes listings that are wheelchair-accessible, have toilets accommodating wheelchairs and are otherwise navigable for those with ambulatory challenges.

NOTES

>INDEX

See also separate subindexes for See (p212), Shop (p213), Eat (p214), Drink (p215) and Play (p215).

SEE

000 map pages

000 map pages

000 map pages